THE MENTAL RESILIENCE METHOD FOR YOUNG ATHLETES

5 SCIENCE-BASED MINDSET TRAINING STRATEGIES TO GAIN CONFIDENCE, IMPROVE FOCUS AND WIN YOUR NEXT GAME

INNER CHAMPION

© **Copyright - Inner Champion 2024 - All rights reserved.**

The content contained within this book may not be reproduced, duplicated, or transmitted without direct written permission from the author or the publisher.

Under no circumstances will any blame or legal responsibility be held against the publisher, or author, for any damages, reparation, or monetary loss due to the information contained within this book, either directly or indirectly. You are responsible for your own choices, actions, and results. Please note the information contained within this document is for educational and entertainment purposes only. All effort has been executed to present accurate, up-to-date, and reliable, complete information.

Legal Notice:

This book is copyright-protected. This book is only for personal use. You cannot amend, distribute, sell, use, quote, or paraphrase any part, or the content within this book, without the consent of the author or publisher.

eBook ISBN: 978-1-915710-56-7

Paperback ISBN: 978-1-915710-57-4

Hardcover ISBN: 978-1-915710-58-1

Published by: Inner Champion

TABLE OF CONTENTS

Preface — 5
Foreword — 7
Introduction — 9

1. THE GAME WITHIN — 15
   The Amazing Mind-Body Connection — 16
   The Resilience Factor — 21
   The Science Behind Mental Resilience — 24
   Mental Resilience in Action — 27
   The Ripple Effect: Beyond the Game — 31

2. FINDING YOUR FOCUS — 35
   Strategy #1: Harness the Power of Mindfulness — 36
   Discover the Mindful Athlete Within — 39
   How Mindfulness Enhances Your Sports Performance — 42
   Mindfulness and Meditation in Action — 44
   The Playbook: Harnessing Your Inner Strength — 45
   Mindfulness and Meditation Apps You Can Use — 50

3. SEE IT; ACHIEVE IT — 55
   Strategy #2: Visualize Your Desired Outcomes — 56
   Seeing it in Your Mind — 58
   How Does Visualization Work? — 62
   Visualization in Action — 66
   The Playbook: Crafting Your Vision — 67

4. KEEP YOUR COOL — 73
   Strategy #3: Master Your Emotions — 74
   Conquering Your Inner Game — 75
   The Science of Riding the Wave — 79
   Emotional Regulation in Action — 83
   The Playbook: Strategies for Winning the Mental Game — 85

5. DESTINATION: VICTORY ... 93
   Strategy #4: Set Strategic Goals ... 93
   Why Goals Matter ... 98
   The Science Behind Goal Setting ... 100
   Goal-Setting in Action ... 101
   The Playbook: Setting Goals and Tracking Progress ... 104

6. THE CHAMPION'S MIND ... 109
   Strategy #5: Cultivate a Growth Mindset ... 110
   Growth Mindset and Resilience ... 114
   How Having a Growth Mindset Boosts Your Game ... 118
   Growth Mindset in Action ... 119
   The Playbook: Kickstarting Your Mindset Makeover ... 121

7. FOR PARENTS: SHAPING THE CHAMPIONS OF TOMORROW ... 129
   Your Role as Parents ... 129
   Parents Behind the Success ... 132
   Nurturing Emotional Well-Being and Fostering Mental Resilience ... 136

   Conclusion ... 143
   References ... 145

Join our email list to get notified about future releases and get free copies of our books.
Scan the QR code to join.

FOREWORD

Since I started my career in the field of psychology, there has not been a single moment when I did not find the need to educate my clients about the importance of the mind-body connection. The power of this connection is vastly underappreciated, yet when properly utilized, its impact is profound, affecting not only sports but every aspect of life. The team at Inner Champion has committed to imparting wisdom on how to build and integrate this power into sporting performance and everyday life.

It is a fact that the youth are the most vulnerable population, and we must help them build mental resilience. The risk of adverse psychological effects increases when young people feel the weight of expectation over their athletic performance. The critical task to avoid this lies in training a healthy, positive, and full-of-strength mindset. This "can do" attitude, essential when trying to reach maximum potential in an athletic setting, is explored and dissected in this book.

Many of my patients have struggled with financial issues, family problems, and other taxing responsibilities, and it is too often forgotten that 'self' and 'health' should be the priority. This book is a self-help manual for those seeking a coach to help them balance their passionate sporting energy with an optimal mind-body connection. Emotional regulation, the parents' role in success, and the ripple effect strengthening your mind has on your whole life are the topics that I believe hold the greatest influence over the success of a young athlete.

So, my keen readers, it is time to finally utilize the resources you already hold within. I, on behalf of Inner Champion, welcome you to become a master of your upcoming success. Own your sense of freedom in choosing a healthier mind and body every day, and elevate yourself to the performance you desire!

We trust in you and wish you endless sporting success.

Dr. Nazish Idrees Chaudhary
Registered Clinical Psychologist & Certified Psychotherapist, PhD

INTRODUCTION

What if I invited you on a journey that's about to revolutionize your game–not just on the field but in every pivotal moment that defines you? I get it. You're not just here to play; you're here to dominate. You've got the talent, the drive, and the heart, but something is missing in those high-stakes moments that keeps you from truly shining. I've been there too, and I'm here to tell you that it's not your skills that need refining–it's your mindset.

Let's talk about legends for a moment–athletes who didn't just rise to the occasion but owned it. Take Michael Jordan, for example. Widely hailed as a basketball deity, he had his share of dark days. I'm talking about that moment in high school when he was cut from the varsity team, considered too short to make the cut. Imagine the frustration, the tears. But what sets legends like him apart is what they do with those setbacks.

You've been there too, haven't you? The crunch time, the pressure cooker moments that have the power to make or break you. Maybe you've felt the weight of expectation, the eyes of your team, coaches, and fans on you, and deep down, the fear of not measuring up. I've been right where you are, grappling with the nerves that sabotage even the most polished skills. But here's the truth that can change everything–it's not about eliminating the pressure; it's about harnessing it.

The reason you picked up this book? It's not just a desire; it's a hunger. A hunger to perform at your best when the stakes are sky-high, to rise above the doubt and seize those moments that define champions. You see, the true game-changer isn't a new drill or a magical technique; it's your mind, your mental resiliency.

In these pages, you'll find science-fueled strategies battle-tested by athletes who turned their doubts into determination and vulnerabilities into victories. You're not alone on this journey; you're joining a league of those who dared to confront their fears and rewrite their stories.

Imagine stepping onto that court, that track, or that field with a heart that doesn't race with anxiety but pulses with confidence. Envision yourself in that pivotal moment, the clock ticking down, the crowd roaring, and you? You're in your element, a force to be reckoned with. This isn't about winning every match; it's about winning the match against self-doubt.

So, let's be honest–you're not here to read a book; you're here to unlock your potential. You're here to transform those moments of pressure into platforms of performance. You're here to elevate your game, not just for the game's sake but for the life you'll lead beyond it.

The surprising thing is that for every elite athlete or Olympian you admire, 80% of their ability and achievements are tied to mental resiliency. Mental resiliency helps them figure out what matters to them so that they can put their focus there so as not to be overstretched. It helps them see and visualize their goals and keep cool on their way to athletic success.

Here, you'll discover that mental resiliency helps you win the game within so that any game you play outside is already pre-won in the ways that matter most. This is a journey to build a champion's mind.

Imagine a life where you walk onto the field with a heart unburdened by anxiety, where you play your best game, win or lose, and still hold your head high. Picture yourself enjoying the freedom to explore other passions to experience life beyond the confines of the sports arena. It's not a fantasy; it's within your grasp.

It's a fact that a lack of mental resiliency is the biggest enemy of athletes. It causes them to give in, give up, tank the match, and give less. I would go so far as to say that your athletic success is directly proportional to your resilience. And to be resilient involves coping with adversity. Mental resiliency is an attitude, and attitudes are created by you and no one else. If you are responsible for your attitudes, you can deconstruct how you think about yourself and others and your ability to succeed. You can change how you think, how you feel about yourself, and how you act, train, and compete. You can learn to manage stress better, stay focused on and off the field, and bounce back faster when encountering setbacks. You can feel more confident about who you are, less anxious, and more in control, not only in your sport but in life.

That is the better way I am offering you in this book. I want to help you build the habit of mental resiliency. I call it a habit because mental resiliency is not something you will pull out of your back pocket when you have seconds left in a game or need to win a tournament. It will undoubtedly help then, but mental resiliency will require an ironclad approach to the challenges in your sporting life consistently. You will need to focus and grow it so that when it becomes a habit, you can consistently perform at the upper range of your athletic ability. You become better equipped to deal with obstacles, interferences, and challenging circumstances without losing motivation or confidence.

Mental resiliency is like your fitness level. The more you train, the fitter you become. When you stop training, your fitness level slips back. Without consistent attendance to your mental fitness, your mental resiliency level will start to atrophy. Resilience is not an all-or-nothing proposition. There are varying degrees, but it is true that as your mental resiliency reserves increase, you will see your athletic performance grow. That is why I have provided actionable techniques at the end of each chapter. My goal is to help you not only understand the concepts but put them into practice.

In this book, I will introduce five strategies to train your mindset for elite athletic performance. You will find stories of men and women actively using each strategy to show you evidence that they work. I will present you with scientific data to back the anecdotal evidence; then, I will hold your hand as you put them into practice.

And do you want to know the good news? You can put these strategies into place immediately and start seeing results straight away. Yes, you read that correctly. These tools are so powerful you can start seeing results that quickly. If you practice them consistently and for long enough, the results can be massive.

If you are courageous enough to be trained by the wisdom of this book, you will undoubtedly be on your way to making your mark in your sport without hurting the other aspects of your life.

With a blend of psychology, experienced athletes, and passionate writers, the Inner Champion team combines deep scientific insights and real-world experience with a singular goal in mind: to unlock the potential of young athletes through the power of mental toughness. This book captures our commitment to the well-being and development of young sportspeople. Through extensive research, innovative writing, and an intuitive understanding of the young athlete's journey, Inner Champion explores the world of sports psychology in a practical and accessible way. Our work sheds light on the often-overlooked mental aspects of sports, providing young athletes with the tools they need to succeed not just on the field but in life.

We firmly believe in the positive impact of sports on young people's lives, so we strive to educate and inspire. Our writings testify that physical ability alone does not define an athlete's potential; instead, it's the inner strength that truly creates champions. We write for young athletes. We write for coaches and parents. We write to offer strategies to foster growth, resilience, and a winning mindset firmly grounded in science and extensive research. We are dedicated to continuous learning and knowledge dissemination so that Inner Champion is not just a name but a mission: to help every young athlete discover and harness the power of their inner champion.

As such, this book is not just about building mental resilience for the sake of sport; it is about transforming your entire approach to life. As you become a master of mental strength, you will uncover a newfound sense of self-belief and resilience that will transcend the boundaries of your athletic endeavors and permeate every aspect of your existence.

So, are you ready to unlock your full potential? Are you prepared to step onto the path of mental resilience that transforms not just your sports performance but your entire life? This book is your ticket to self-discovery, growth, and victory.

CHAPTER 1
THE GAME WITHIN

Whenever we witness exceptional athletes in action, it's easy to be captivated by their awe-inspiring physical abilities. The strength, speed, and agility on display are truly remarkable. However, digging a little deeper, we uncover a fascinating truth: what separates a good athlete from a genuinely great one often goes beyond physical prowess. The real game-changer, the secret ingredient that propels champions to extraordinary heights, is something less visible but equally potent–mental strength.

In this chapter, we will look into mental resilience in sports. We will explore the pivotal role that psychological readiness plays in achieving athletic excellence. It's not just about physical fitness; it's about cultivating a robust mindset that can withstand the challenges, the setbacks, and the intense pressure that comes with pursuing greatness. Throughout this chapter, we will uncover compelling insights backed by scientific research that reveal the significance of mental resilience in shaping the destiny of athletes.

THE AMAZING MIND-BODY CONNECTION

Our minds and bodies are not as separate as we might think. Everything we think up in our minds directly impacts how our bodies feel. Whether we realize it or not, the connection between mind and body is vital in our daily lives. Our thoughts, feelings, beliefs, and attitudes can be our best friends or our nemeses regarding our biological functioning. That means our minds can boost our overall health or drag us down.

And guess what? It goes both ways. How we treat our physical bodies, from what we eat to how much we move and even how we carry ourselves, can have a massive effect on our mental state. It's like a two-way street, with our minds and bodies chatting and influencing each other in this fascinating dance. For clarity, when we say "mind," we're not just talking about our brains. It's so much more. Our minds encompass all those mental states like thoughts, emotions, beliefs, attitudes, and even those vivid mental images we conjure up. The brain is like the hardware that allows us to experience this whirlwind of mental activity.

Sometimes, our mental states are like ninjas–they can be fully conscious or hidden in the shadows of our subconscious. We might react emotionally to stuff without realizing why we feel that way. And guess what? Each of these mental states has a physical impact on our bodies. So, when you're feeling anxious, your body's like, "Hey, let's release some stress hormones!" As a biologist would explain, when we encounter something stressful, our brains kick into action and trigger a whole chain of reactions in our bodies. It's like a domino effect.

First, our sympathetic nervous system (SNS) goes into fight, flight, or freeze mode, preparing us to deal with the threat. Our 'superhero' adrenal glands rescue us, releasing stress hormones like adrenaline and noradrenaline, giving us that extra energy boost. The hypothalamic-pituitary-adrenal axis gets in on the action too, which triggers the release of another stress hormone called cortisol. All these hormones working together make our heart race, our breathing go wild, and send the blood rushing away from "maintenance" stuff, like digestion, to our arms and legs in case we need to bolt or battle.

As if that wasn't enough, our brain shifts gears, moving the focus from logical thinking to more emotional and survival-related responses. It's like a high-speed switch in the brain. Now, here's where things can get tricky. When we face stress a lot, whether from constantly challenging situations or how we perceive things, our "fight, flight, freeze" mode can become a regular occurrence, putting us into chronic stress, which can do a number on our bodies. The stress hormones that save the day in emergencies can become troublesome when they keep circulating in our system. Our immunity gets suppressed, inflammation becomes a problem we must deal with, and proinflammatory cytokines (a group of messengers released in the body when it is under threat) begin to make us feel down and tired, making it hard to stay on top of healthy habits like exercise. Over time, all this chronic stress can lead to many physical problems. It's like our bodies are practically telling us to take it easy.

The mind-body connection is not a new idea. Around 300 years ago, almost every medicine system worldwide saw the mind and body as a team working together. But things took a turn during the 17th century when the Western world started viewing them as separate entities. According to this new perspective, the body was like a machine with replaceable, separate parts without connection to the mind.

Don't get it wrong–this Western viewpoint had some perks. It paved the way for incredible advancements in trauma care, surgery, pharmaceuticals, and other areas of modern medicine. But here's the thing–it put the brakes on exploring humans' emotional and spiritual side and underestimated our natural ability to heal. Fast forward to the 20th century, and things began to shift. Researchers started to study the mind-body connection more seriously and found some mind-blowing stuff. They discovered that the body and mind are best buddies with a deep, intricate bond.

Integrative psychiatrist James Lake from Stanford University says it best: "Extensive research confirms the medical and mental benefits of mindfulness training, meditation, yoga, and other mind-body practices." There's way more to this mind-body connection than meets the eye. As science delves deeper into it, we uncover the powerful ways our thoughts, emotions, and practices like meditation and mindfulness can impact our overall well-being. It's a whole new understanding of how our minds and bodies team up to keep us healthy and happy.

The mind and body connection also plays a role in athletic success. People often ask, which factor wields more significant influence over a performer's achievements–the body or the mind? At first glance, an athlete's performance may seem solely dependent on their physical attributes, with peak athleticism manifesting through explosive movements and powerful bodies. However, their mental state is just as pivotal in their performance.

Imagine an athlete who sees their performances to fall short of their true potential and asks for help to improve their game. Determining whether the challenges they face originate from their mind or body isn't a straightforward task. We often want binary answers that divide the physical and mental aspects of sports into distinct entities, ignoring their inseparable connection, which is the true catalyst for success or failure.

According to research from Johns Hopkins University, the mind-body connection entails the belief that the causes, development, and outcomes of physical illnesses and poor performance are influenced by an intricate interplay of psychological, social, and biological factors. Embracing this definition removes the need to assign blame solely on physical skills or mental fortitude when an athlete underperforms. Instead, a more holistic approach considers the athlete a whole human being.

If the mind and body are connected, then to reach peak performance, you cannot focus solely on honing physical skills; nurturing a strong and healthy mind is equally indispensable. While physical training remains crucial, mental training will unlock your full potential. Think about someone experiencing performance anxiety. Anxiety has a tangible impact on physical performance, causing the body to become tense and rigid, hampering speed and flexibility. Despite honing physical skills through relentless practice, their performance can suffer when the mind impedes the athlete's free expression of talent on the big stage.

In the same way, your self-image will affect your athletic performance. How we perceive ourselves holds tremendous power, impacting athletic performance positively or negatively. Self-image here encompasses more than just our outward appearance; it involves how we see ourselves in all aspects of life. In athletics, self-image influences our perception of success, how we handle anxiety, our performance under pressure, and our confidence level. There's a well-known saying, "You cannot outperform your self-image." If you believe you perform poorly under pressure, that image will likely align with your performance. While occasional strokes of luck may occur, your self-image profoundly affects your abilities.

We cannot discuss the mind and body connection in sports without touching on our emotions. The mind is a powerful tool that can elevate athletic performance but can be a hindrance if left unchecked. Our emotions directly stem from the thoughts in our minds and profoundly influence our behaviors. In an ideal world, we would master our emotions and use them as assets. However, many of us find ourselves at their mercy. In turn, these emotions drive our on-field actions. Negative emotions can detrimentally impact performance, whereas managing emotions positively can be advantageous.

The mind-body connection is already present, influencing us even if we do not realize it. The question is whether we can learn to strengthen this connection to enhance its positive impact on athletic performance. This means gaining more control over our thought processes and emotions.

THE RESILIENCE FACTOR

Resilience is the ability to handle challenging events and bounce back from adversity. It refers to an individual's capacity to handle and recover from difficult events effectively. It is the ability to remain flexible in thoughts, feelings, and behaviors when confronted with disruptions or prolonged periods of pressure, ultimately emerging from difficulties stronger, wiser, and more capable. While everyone is born with a certain degree of personal resilience, this trait may vary throughout one's life, influenced by age, gender, and past experiences. The good news is that you can actively enhance your mental resilience.

"Mental toughness" is often used interchangeably with resilience, but research highlights subtle differences. Mental toughness is described as resilience combined with confidence, representing an offensive strategy to prevent being knocked down in the first place. In contrast, resilience is a defensive strategy to help people get back up when pushed down.

The resilient person does not simply bounce back from adversity. Significant life events, like the loss of a loved one or a severe medical diagnosis, can lead even the most resilient individuals to new life paths. Psychology recognizes that resilient people often experience growth and transformation after dark times. These transformations can manifest in several ways. For starters, the resilient person could discover unexpected abilities as they face and overcome each new challenge, leading to a more empowered self-perception. Secondly, during difficult times, resilient people recognize and prioritize positive relationships while identifying and sometimes ending toxic or unsupportive connections, and finally, resilient people come out of difficulties with changed priorities. Challenging circumstances can prompt a re-evaluation of life goals and values, leading to a more focused and meaningful perspective.

A resilient person will overcome a difficult situation with a renewed sense of purpose. This renewed sense of purpose makes them even more so resilient. Studies show that having a clear and valued purpose and fully committing to a mission can significantly strengthen resilience. A renewed sense of purpose can be a guiding force, helping you navigate through adversity with determination and resilience. Resilience research highlights different key factors that both facilitate and indicate resilience in people:

- **Reframing**: Viewing problems or situations from a different, more constructive perspective can significantly aid coping mechanisms. Reframing challenges allows you to find helpful solutions and navigate difficulties more easily.
- **Relying on positive emotions**: Harnessing the power of positive emotions has a transformative effect on resilience. Such emotions broaden thinking and enable you to develop creative strategies for problem-solving. Additionally, they foster a sense of belonging and facilitate strong connections with supportive people and groups, fostering feelings of accomplishment and purposeful living.
- **Getting physically active**: Participation in physical activities plays a crucial role in managing and reducing stress. It boosts confidence and self-esteem,

empowering people to face challenges with increased resilience.
- **Having a community around you**: Ongoing active engagement in trusted social networks offers vital social support. Support from friends, colleagues, and family members helps you feel less isolated and encourages you to adopt a more positive perspective on life events.
- **Using your strengths**: Recognizing and utilizing your signature strengths profoundly impacts resilience. Participating in activities that align with personal strengths fosters a sense of authenticity, enhances meaning in life, and instills a sense of control when confronting new challenges or adversities.
- **Staying optimistic**: Adopting a hopeful outlook toward the future is a potent resilience booster. An optimistic mindset allows you to see setbacks as temporary and surmountable, creating a sense of hope and positivity for what lies ahead.

As athletes, we face many challenges in our sporting careers, ranging from competitive pressures and organizational demands to personal stressors from our non-sporting lives. These stressors can lead to setbacks, adversities, and obstacles, including injuries, underperformance, abuse, and mental health concerns. In such situations, having high resilience becomes crucial to withstand pressure, recover from setbacks, and achieve success. We need resilience during injury rehabilitation. It helps us to overcome negative emotions. After an injury, resilient athletes can maintain a positive mindset, making recovery easier.

Resilience also helps athletes cope with the psychological aspects of sports and the accompanying challenges, such as fear, frustration, and doubt. It keeps them actively engaged, even during rehabilitation. Compared to athletes with low resilience, those with high resilience recover faster from injuries. They are more likely to adhere to the rehabilitation program, which ensures better outcomes. Resilient athletes can effectively deal with setbacks encountered during rehabilitation, maintaining their focus and determination to return to sport.

Resilient athletes exhibit various characteristics that contribute to coping with stressors and adversity. These characteristics include positivity, determination, competitiveness, commitment, maturity, persistence, passion for the sport, strong social support networks, easy temperament, good self-esteem, planning skills, and supportive environments inside and outside the family. Additionally, traits like hope, extraversion, optimism, spirituality, and self-efficacy contribute to their resilience.

THE SCIENCE BEHIND MENTAL RESILIENCE

Recent scientific studies shed light on the vital link between resilience and sports achievement, mental health, and performance. One study investigated the connection between resilience, sports achievement, and mental health in a group of athletes. The results revealed that athletes with higher levels of resilience tended to achieve more tremendous success in their respective sports. Moreover, they reported better mental health and well-being than athletes with lower resilience. Imagine resilience as your mental armor. When you have strong mental resilience, it's like wearing a shield that protects you from negative thoughts and helps you bounce back from setbacks faster. This study shows that athletes with this strong shield perform better in their sports and feel happier and more balanced.

In a different study, researchers explored the psychological traits that underpin resilience in Olympic champions. The findings revealed vital characteristics such as optimism, determination, passion for their sport, and strong social support networks. These champions exhibited a never-give-up attitude and were highly motivated to overcome challenges. Imagine Olympic champions as real-life superheroes. They have unique mental abilities that keep them going, no matter what obstacles they face. These abilities include staying positive, never losing sight of their goals, and having friends and family who support and believe in them. Just like superheroes, these champions use their mental powers to achieve extraordinary feats in their sports.

A different group of scientists wanted to discover why some athletes recover after a major failure while others never do. This study examined how an athlete's explanatory style (which refers to how they interpret and explain failures) relates to their resilience. Athletes with an optimistic explanatory style tended to show greater resilience after facing sports failures. They were more likely to view setbacks as temporary and specific to certain situations rather than personal shortcomings. Think of your explanatory style as the story you tell yourself after a challenging game or competition. Optimistic athletes tell themselves positive stories like, "I had a bad day, but I can improve next time." This way, they don't let one bad game define them. They stay strong and ready for the next challenge.

The same researchers also wanted to understand how athletes bounce back after failure. They explored how coping style, social support, and self-concept influence an athlete's resilience and ability to bounce back after setbacks. Athletes who used positive coping strategies, had a robust support system, and maintained a positive self-concept demonstrated higher levels of resilience in their sports performances. Coping strategies are like tools in your mental toolkit. Athletes who use positive tools, like focusing on what they can control and seeking help from coaches or friends, are better equipped to bounce back. Having supportive people around you, like coaches, teammates, and family, also provides the motivation and encouragement you need to stay strong.

These scientific studies provide valuable insights into the significance of mental resilience in sports. Young athletes can learn from these findings and understand that building resilience is as essential as physical training. Besides, participating in sports can help you to build resilience.

In recent years, the link between sports and positive mental health has drawn significant attention from researchers, mental health professionals, and athletes alike. Engaging in sporting activities has been recognized as a potent resilience factor, particularly in reducing deterioration among people with existing mental illness. The undeniable impact of sports on mental well-being warrants a deeper exploration into how we define and measure both sports participation and positive mental health, to grasp their relationship fully.

Sporting activities, whether competitive or recreational, have proven to be more than just physical exercise. They offer many benefits for mental well-being, making them a valuable tool in maintaining and improving overall mental health. Participating in sports has been linked to reduced symptoms of anxiety and depression, enhanced mood and self-esteem, increased cognitive function, and better stress management. Sports can serve as a powerful coping mechanism for people struggling with mental health challenges. Physical activity releases endorphins, the feel-good chemicals in the brain, which can lead to a sense of euphoria and relief from negative emotions. Besides, being part of a sports team or community fosters social connections and a sense of belonging, further contributing to improved mental health.

Sporting activity and having a trusted adult relationship are essential in preventing the worsening of mental illness symptoms. Engaging in sports gives you a sense of purpose, achievement, and a structured routine, which is vital in building resilience against stress and mental health issues. Athletes, in particular, exhibit remarkable resilience traits due to their constant exposure to challenges and setbacks in their sports careers. Overcoming failures, injuries, and performance pressures hones their mental toughness, enabling them to face life's difficulties with greater strength and determination.

MENTAL RESILIENCE IN ACTION

Everywhere you look, whether in tennis or basketball, among men or women, you will see stories of people who have used their mental resilience to do the extraordinary.

Think about Serena Williams for a moment. From a very early age, she had a passion for the sport and a fierce desire to be the best. As Serena climbed the ranks, she encountered fierce competitors who seemed to stand in her way at every turn. The pressure to perform at her best, fans' expectations, and the media scrutiny took a toll on her mental well-being. She faced defeat and criticism, but Serena refused to be defeated by her doubts and fears. Her resilience shines through major personal setbacks like her parent's divorce in 2002, her sister's killing, and a fair share of heartbreak.

One of the most defining moments in Serena's career came when she suffered a career-threatening knee injury. Doctors warned her that the road to recovery would be long and grueling. Many questioned if she would ever return to her dominant form. But Serena's mental resilience emerged as a guiding light during those dark days of rehabilitation. Instead of giving in to despair, Serena channeled her inner strength, setting small goals for each recovery step. She stayed positive and focused on the things she could control, like her rehabilitation regimen and maintaining a healthy lifestyle. Through perseverance and determination, she returned to the court and regained her position as one of the world's top-ranked players.

Throughout her career, Serena faced criticism and discrimination on and off the court. She was subjected to racial and gender bias but refused to let these external factors define her worth. Instead, Serena turned these challenges into opportunities to inspire change. She advocated for equality in tennis, becoming a powerful voice for social justice and women's rights. Serena displayed remarkable composure in crucial matches, remaining calm and focused despite adversity. Her unwavering self-belief and ability to stay composed under pressure became her trademark.

Another shining example of resilience is Simone Biles. As Simone's talent blossomed, so did the weight of expectation on her shoulders. The pressure to be the best was immense, and the world watched closely as she competed in one championship after another. But she refused to be overwhelmed by the pressure. Instead, she embraced it as a driving force to push herself beyond her limits. You can see her resilience in every competition, but her resilience came out clearly during the 2013 World Championships. In a heartbreaking moment, she experienced a significant setback when she stumbled during one of her routines. The disappointment was palpable, and many wondered if she would ever recover. But her mental resilience proved to be her greatest asset.

Instead of letting self-doubt creep in, Simone used the setback to fuel her determination. She returned to the gym with renewed focus, working tirelessly to perfect her skills. She adopted a positive mindset, acknowledging that setbacks were a natural part of the journey to success. This mental shift helped her overcome the disappointment and propelled her toward even more remarkable achievements.

In basketball, you can see a similar resilience in LeBron James. Financial struggles, constant relocations, and an unstable family life marked LeBron's childhood. To shield him from the harsh realities of their circumstances, his mother, Gloria, encouraged him to embrace sports as an outlet for his emotions. In the local parks, LeBron discovered his passion and purpose.

In the middle of adversity, LeBron used sports as a sanctuary to escape the troubles that plagued him. Basketball and football became more than just games; they were the pillars of his mental resilience. Despite feeling embarrassed about his lifestyle and finding it challenging to make friends, LeBron channeled those emotions into motivation. He sought to prove that his circumstances did not define him; instead, they fueled his determination to rise above them.

LeBron's mental resilience shone brightest on the basketball court. As he honed his skills and talents, he became a formidable force. His unwavering work ethic and commitment to improvement set him apart from his peers. When he came across challenges on the court, he did not crumble under pressure; instead, he rose to the occasion with unparalleled determination. One of the defining moments of LeBron's career came in 2010 when he made the controversial decision to leave his hometown team to join the Miami Heat. The public backlash was immense, with critics questioning his loyalty and character. But LeBron stood firm, believing the move was essential for his growth as a player and a leader.

LeBron's journey eventually led him back to Cleveland, where he fulfilled his promise of delivering a championship to his beloved city. The 2016 NBA Finals became a showcase of his mental resilience. Facing a historic 3-1 deficit against the Golden State Warriors, he refused to back down. He led his team in a stunning comeback, winning the series and earning the title of Finals MVP. Throughout his career, LeBron faced injuries, personal tragedies, and constant scrutiny but never allowed these challenges to deter him. His mental resilience is the bedrock of his success, enabling him to overcome adversity and rise to greatness.

THE RIPPLE EFFECT: BEYOND THE GAME

Mental resilience is a transformative quality that enhances your sporting performance and permeates various aspects of your life. The benefits of resilience extend far beyond the playing field, creating a ripple effect that positively impacts overall well-being and success in many areas, including:

- Reducing the risk of physical illnesses related to stress

Resilient people are better equipped to manage stress effectively. Chronic stress can lead to various physical health issues, such as heart disease, high blood pressure, and weakened immune function. Resilient people reduce the risk of stress-related physical illnesses by healthily handling stress.

- Lowering anxiety

Resilience enables you to face anxiety-inducing situations with a sense of control and confidence. It allows you to develop coping mechanisms that minimize anxiety and maintain emotional stability even in challenging circumstances.

- Reducing depression

Resilience acts as a buffer against depression. People with mental resilience are more likely to recover from setbacks and maintain a positive outlook, which helps prevent depressive symptoms.

- Living longer

The ability to effectively cope with life's ups and downs contributes to improved overall well-being, leading to increased longevity and a healthier lifestyle.

- Reducing high-risk behavior

Resilient people are less prone to engaging in high-risk behaviors as they have strong self-control and can make decisions clearly and rationally.

- Better learning ability

Resilient people have a growth mindset that encourages them to embrace challenges as opportunities for learning and personal growth. This mindset enhances their learning ability and adaptability to new situations.

- Better social ties

Resilient people tend to form stronger social connections. Their ability to handle stress and maintain emotional stability makes them more approachable and supportive, leading to more profound and meaningful relationships. Not only that, but resilience contributes to healthier and more stable long-term relationships. In times of conflict or adversity, resilient people can maintain open communication, empathize with their partners, and work through challenges together.

- Greater success at work

In professional life, resilience is a crucial factor in success. Resilient people are better equipped to handle workplace stress, adapt to changes, and bounce back from setbacks, leading to improved performance and career advancement.

Life is unpredictable, and challenges are inevitable. Resilience equips you with the mental and emotional tools to face the uncertainties of life with courage and adaptability. Mental resilience is a life-changing quality that will make you a better athlete and allow you to thrive in all aspects of life. While resilience helps you endure, what do you do when all eyes are on you, and the pressure is intense? In the next chapter, you will learn how to keep your focus and manage pressure in sports.

CHAPTER 2
FINDING YOUR FOCUS

Picture this: you are in the heart of a high-pressure game situation. All eyes are on you, and the weight of expectations bears down heavily on your shoulders. The tension in the air is palpable, and the stakes couldn't be higher. Yet, amidst the chaos, you exude extraordinary calm and composure. Your mind is focused, your movements deliberate, and your confidence unwavering. How is this level of control even possible? The answer lies in the practices of mindfulness and meditation.

In this chapter, we explore the incredible potential that mindfulness and meditation hold for athletes and sports enthusiasts alike. Far from being abstract mystical concepts, these practices offer concrete and tangible benefits that can significantly impact athletic performance. The pressure of an athletic competition can be overwhelming, affecting even the most seasoned athletes. However, incorporating mindfulness and meditation into your training regimen can unlock hidden reservoirs of mental strength and resilience. These practices cultivate present-moment awareness and a deep connection between mind and body, enabling you to navigate high-pressure situations with unparalleled poise.

But this isn't just a collection of anecdotal evidence; this chapter looks into the scientific research that underpins the effectiveness of mindfulness and meditation in sports. We'll explore how these practices positively influence neural pathways, emotional regulation, and cognitive function, improving focus, concentration, and decision-making. Here, you'll discover practical and science-backed techniques to seamlessly integrate mindfulness and meditation into your daily training routine. If you want to enhance your athletic performance, this chapter will give you the tools to thrive under pressure and achieve peak performance.

STRATEGY #1: HARNESS THE POWER OF MINDFULNESS

Are you mindful, or is your mind just full? Distinguishing between the two is vital, as the mind, while excellent for problem-solving, often struggles to find peace and remain in the present. Instead of residing in the here and now, it frequently wanders to the past or the future, cluttered with thoughts, stories, and narratives that may not be relevant to the current moment. Sometimes, the mind may become entangled in illusions and fiction that lack any basis in reality. This, of course, affects your everyday functioning and your athletic performance. Mindfulness can be a source of refuge from a distracted mind.

A full mind remains detached from the present moment. By nature, our minds think, analyze, and try to decipher things, constantly seeking new stimuli and distractions from the world around us. The mind can pull you further from reality if you are not conscious. A mindful mind does the opposite. Mindfulness involves gently directing your awareness to the present moment. Often, it entails focusing on sensations to anchor yourself in your body and the present reality. You can cultivate mindfulness during formal meditation sessions or everyday activities like cooking, cleaning, or walking.

Mindfulness is a gentle way to retrain the mind, encouraging it to settle into the present moment. In a sense, it's like taking on the role of a parent in your mind rather than letting it dictate your experiences. Ultimately, the mind can be likened to a willful toddler. With the patient and compassionate repetition of mindfulness exercises, you can teach the mind to be still and find tranquility. In time, it may dissolve altogether, leading to a state where no intellectual or conceptual layers separate you from your immediate experiences. This state of actual presence allows you to fully immerse in and be at one with the present moment.

Extensive research has documented the many benefits of mindfulness. The Western world's formal research on mindfulness started in 1979 when John Kabat-Zinn pioneered the Mindfulness-Based Stress Reduction (MBSR) program. Drawing from his expertise in Hatha yoga, mindfulness practices, and Buddhist principles taught by his mentors, Kabat-Zinn laid the foundation for a transformative approach to well-being.

Since then, research into MBSR and general mindfulness has exploded, revealing many advantages for those who practice mindfulness. These benefits encompass a host of improvements in various aspects of life, including cognitive ability, brain health, emotional well-being, and quality of life, among others. Studies have demonstrated that mindfulness can improve cognitive ability, slow brain aging, and even reduce symptoms of stress, anxiety, and depression. People who engage in regular mindfulness practice report a heightened sense of well-being, and those living with chronic conditions find relief and improved quality of life.

Regarding brain health, research has shown that mindfulness meditation can lead to significant changes in brain structure linked to lower depression scores. Long-term meditation practitioners have exhibited slower rates of brain tissue loss, particularly in areas responsible for mood regulation and emotional/cognitive integration. Mindfulness has also shown its efficacy in increasing well-being, reducing stress, and enhancing job satisfaction. It has been found effective in treating anxiety symptoms, even in younger populations, and has been hailed as a cost-effective complementary approach to anxiety treatment.

So far, we have mentioned meditation alongside mindfulness, so it pays to define it. Meditation is a skill that helps you to be mindful and redirect your attention to the present moment. Learning how to meditate is a lot like learning any other skill. It is like exercising a muscle group. It will take some time to get comfortable with it, and it is easier if you are consistent and have guidance. As you learn how to meditate, it is worth remembering that it is meditation practice and won't be perfect. Sometimes, your focus will wander, and that is acceptable. It is part of the experience. The important thing is to stay consistent. Consistency matters more than the destination.

DISCOVER THE MINDFUL ATHLETE WITHIN

To better understand the place of mindfulness in sports, let's step into the mind of an incredible athlete, like an Olympic sailor. She's been training hard for years to achieve her dream of winning an Olympic medal. Now, she's in the lead at the Olympics, but the competition is fierce, and the final race will decide her fate. On the morning of the final race, she knows exactly what she needs to do to win. Stay focused on the present moment, observe the winds, and sail with good technique. But she's nervous because, in the past, she's lost the lead at critical moments. As the race begins, she gets a shaky start, and doubts about her previous losses start creeping in.

Her mind wanders, thinking about the past and worrying about the future. This distraction makes her miss important things happening in the race. Luckily, she realizes her focus isn't right, bringing her attention back to the present. She faces many distractions during the race—sometimes, she gets ahead of herself, imagining victory, and other times, she worries about what could go wrong. But every time her mind wanders, she notices it and returns it to the present moment. This is a skill she's been practicing a lot. Despite her distractions, she keeps reminding herself of her strategy and ultimately wins a medal.

You might think that athletes like her are always focused, but just like anyone else, they struggle with distractions too. Our minds have extraordinary powers, but they can also lead us astray. We often think about our past mistakes or worry about what might happen. Athletes face much pressure, especially during events like the Olympics, where success means so much to them. But staying focused can be challenging when the outcome is uncertain. However, our sailor has the secret weapon of mindfulness.

Mindfulness is like a superpower that helps her refocus whenever her mind wanders. When her mind wanders, she begins by registering that it has happened, releasing the distracting thoughts, and then refocusing on the task. It's a skill she's honed through practice, just like her sailing techniques. Mindfulness helps her stay present, even in nerve-wracking situations. This is what mindfulness can do for you too.

Mindfulness enhances focus, reduces stress, and promotes overall well-being. Its potential, however, extends far beyond meditation cushions and peaceful retreats; it profoundly impacts the world of sports. The mindful athlete recognizes that success isn't solely determined by physical abilities but also by mental fortitude. In high-pressure game situations, staying composed and calm can make the difference between winning and defeat. By cultivating mindfulness, you can sharpen your focus, silence distractions, and access a flow state—an optimal mental state where performance reaches its peak.

Mindfulness empowers you to remain rooted in the present, resisting the temptation to dwell on past mistakes or fear future outcomes. Instead of being consumed by nerves or self-doubt, you learn to accept and acknowledge your thoughts and emotions without being overwhelmed. This newfound mental clarity fosters resilience, allowing you to recover from failure and keep a positive attitude.

You may be wondering why staying in the moment is a good thing, especially when the moment is a high-pressure sporting environment. Well, being present will boost your performance. It gives you super focus so that all your energy goes into playing and playing well. You become aware of your actions and execute them better. In that state, you are no longer competing with distractions. The anxious feelings during the game no longer hold much sway over you. You can relax, and as a result, your movements are smoother and faster. Mindfulness and meditation will allow you to enjoy the following benefits:

- **Super focus**: Imagine you're shooting a free throw in basketball. If your mind isn't focused, you might miss the shot. Meditation trains your brain to stay focused, helping you perform better in any sport.
- **Pain relief**: Athletes often deal with aches and pains from demanding sports. Meditation can help you cope with pain and feel better.
- **Fear buster**: Fears can mess up your game, but meditation can calm that fear center in your brain, even when you're not meditating. It will give you the ability to face challenges fearlessly.
- **Thought tamer**: After a tough loss or failure, we get stuck in negative thoughts. Meditation helps us stop overthinking and focus on the present moment.
- **Resilience booster**: The greatest athletes bounce back from failures, and meditation can help you become more resilient. It's all about detaching from negative thoughts and reaching your goals.

- **Stress relief**: Athletes deal with lots of stress, but meditation can calm you down and make you more relaxed before a game.
- **Emotional stability**: Sports can be an emotional roller coaster, but meditation helps you control your feelings and stay steady.
- **Better sleep**: Quality sleep is crucial for athletes, and meditation can improve your sleep so you're ready for game day.

HOW MINDFULNESS ENHANCES YOUR SPORTS PERFORMANCE

Mindfulness is not just for Zen masters or meditation gurus. It has found its way into the world of sports and is proving to be a game-changer for athletes of all levels. Mindfulness enhances sports performance by sharpening focus, reducing stress, and improving mental and physical well-being. Picture this: you are standing on the basketball court, the crowd roaring, and the pressure mounting. Your mind starts racing about the last shot you missed or the upcoming game-winning attempt. This mental clutter can hinder your ability to focus on the present moment and lead to costly mistakes.

Mindfulness helps you stay in the zone by training your mind to let go of distractions and fully engage with the task. Practicing mindfulness enables you to observe your thoughts without getting tangled in them. As a result, you become more present during practice and competition, allowing you to react instinctively to every movement and respond swiftly to changing game situations.

It also helps you to manage stress. Stress is inevitable in sports, but excessive stress can adversely impact performance. When stressed, your body tenses up, and your mind becomes clouded with worries and fears. This can cause poor decision-making and a decline in overall performance. Mindfulness acts as a powerful stress-reduction tool. By regularly practicing mindfulness techniques, athletes can lower their stress levels and gain better control over their emotions. This improved emotional regulation helps them maintain composure under pressure, enabling them to make clear-headed decisions and perform at their best when it matters most.

In sports, setbacks and failures are inevitable. A missed shot, a lost match, or an injury can leave athletes feeling demoralized and discouraged. However, athletes who practice mindfulness develop greater mental resilience, enabling them to bounce back from disappointments and stay motivated to keep pushing forward. Mindfulness teaches you to embrace a non-judgmental attitude toward your performance. Instead of criticizing yourself for mistakes, you learn to see setbacks as a chance to grow and learn. This positive mindset empowers you to persevere through challenges and return even stronger.

The icing on the cake is that mindfulness increases your body awareness. For an athlete, body awareness is essential for precise movements and coordination. Mindfulness practice heightens your ability to connect with your body. You become more attuned to your posture, muscle tension, and breathing patterns. This heightened body awareness allows you to make subtle adjustments to your movements, leading to improved technique and reduced risk of injuries. Besides, being in tune with your body helps you recognize early signs of fatigue and take necessary rest, ultimately supporting your long-term performance and overall well-being.

MINDFULNESS AND MEDITATION IN ACTION

The benefits of mindfulness and meditation are not only celebrated in academia. Many renowned athletes practice mindfulness, which has helped them be better performers. Athletic greats Barry Zito, Joe Namath, and Arthur Ashe have praised meditation as a tool for athletic success. Even entire teams have been embracing visualization and mindfulness practices. Kobe Bryant, Derek Jeter, LeBron James, Misty May-Treanor and Kerri Walsh, Michael Jordan, and Ricky Williams all practice mindfulness. Even Phil Jackson has a mindfulness approach to basketball.

The legendary NBA coach, Phil Jackson, is known for his unique approach to the game, incorporating mindfulness and Zen-style philosophies into his coaching methods. He has an impressive record of 11 NBA Championship rings, 6 with the Chicago Bulls and 5 with the Los Angeles Lakers, and is widely considered one of the greatest coaches in the history of the NBA. Throughout his coaching career, Jackson worked with basketball superstars like Michael Jordan, Scottie Pippen, Shaquille O'Neal, and Kobe Bryant. He earned the nickname "The Zen Master" and was inducted into the Basketball Hall of Fame due to his impact on the game through his graceful style.

In one instance, Jackson organized basketball clinics on South Dakota's Pine Ridge Reservation, where he learned about Sioux Lakota practices and incorporated their leadership values into his coaching and personal life. His connection with players extends beyond the court. For example, he bonded with Dennis Rodman through Native American culture. Rodman felt understood and accepted by Jackson, strengthening their relationship and the team's unity. He couldn't have done this without mindfulness.

It is said that the coach's mindfulness techniques were unique and intriguing to players. He would give handpicked books to inspire individual players and use sage in the locker room to break losing streaks. He encouraged meditation to help players stay present and focused, free from outside worries and distractions. Using the concept of "one breath, one mind," he taught his teams to approach problems with open minds and concentrate on the task at hand.

Phil Jackson's coaching legacy lives on through former players turned coaches, such as Steve Kerr, Luke Walton, and Brian Shaw, who have incorporated elements of Jackson's style into their coaching methods. His contribution to basketball is remarkable, and most of his achievements owe to embracing mindfulness.

THE PLAYBOOK: HARNESSING YOUR INNER STRENGTH

The following are mindfulness exercises and practices that can get you started and keep you focused. Remember that mindfulness is most effective when you practice it regularly. Sometimes, it will feel like a lot of work to attach yourself to a new habit. Keep at it. A good rule of thumb is to identify the type of mindfulness you enjoy and figure out how to make it sustainable.

1. Deep breathing

Deep breathing is a classic mindfulness activity where you focus on your breath. It's about taking slow, deep breaths using your belly (diaphragm). This helps your body relax and feel more at ease. All you need is to spare ten uninterrupted minutes of your day. The best time is in the morning before beginning your day or at the end of the day. Sit with your back straight and make yourself comfortable. You can set a timer if you like and close your eyes. Bring your attention to everything around you, notice the room temperature and sounds around you, and then bring your attention to your breath.

At this point, you can count your breaths with the inhalation and exhalation, counting from one until you reach ten. Start again whenever you get distracted. Notice how it feels to breathe in and out. Concentrate on when your breath changes from inhalation to exhalation. If you get distracted, that is alright; just pick up where you left off. The goal is to notice whenever you get distracted and gently bring your attention back to your breath.

2. Paced breathing

Another way to practice mindfulness is through paced breathing. You deliberately control the length of your inhales and exhales. A longer exhalation than an inhalation is good because it slows your heart rate slightly. Give it a shot—breathe in for five counts and breathe out for seven counts. And remember to breathe from your belly. Again, if you get distracted, gently bring your attention back to the task at hand.

3. Grounding with 5-4-3-2-1

The 5-4-3-2-1 grounding exercise uses your senses to return to the present moment. This is how to do it:

- Find five things you can see (maybe pick a color, like five blue things).
- Notice four sensations you can feel, like your back against a chair or the cool air on your hands.
- Listen for three sounds around you.
- Sniff out two things you can smell (it's okay to actively smell things, like the laundry detergent on your clothes).
- Finally, find one thing you can taste. Take a moment to notice the taste.

4. Body scan

A body scan is a simple exercise to help you relax and be acutely aware of how you are feeling right now. The idea is to focus on different parts of your body, spending 10-30 seconds on each part. Start with your toes, then move on to the bottoms and tops of your feet, and so on, moving all the way up your body. Feel all the sensations–warmth, coolness, tension, tingling, pressure, pain, textures, and more. If you reach a body part that feels tense, release the pressure. Once you have scanned through your whole body, you should have released all tension and pressure from your muscles, and you will be more in touch with how your body feels.

5. Meditation

There are different types of meditation, most of which involve keeping one position and maintaining your attention on one thing, like physical sensations, a place, or your breath. Whenever your mind wanders, as it inevitably will, do not judge yourself. Instead, bring your focus back to the point of attention. Remember that it may take a while for meditation to feel comfortable. Try other mindfulness activities or experiment with different types of meditation until you find one that feels easier for you. That said, here are five types of meditation you can try:

- Thought hunter

Watch for any thoughts, however small, and call out the thought to yourself in your head. Be honest with yourself so that you do not let any thought pass. The idea is to learn to be more aware of your thoughts. The thoughts that we are unaware of push us to specific actions that we would otherwise not do if they were conscious thoughts. Do this for three minutes first and adjust the time as you see fit.

- Counting meditation

Sit comfortably or lie on your back and begin counting in your mind from 100 backward. The goal is to get to 1. Counting backward requires that you concentrate and will help you stay focused. Try to keep your mind on the numbers. In case you lose count, start again. If you reach 1, remain silent for a few moments. This exercise is excellent for helping you concentrate; if you can reach one without any distractions, you will have a relaxing experience.

- Counting your thoughts

Imagine your thoughts as objects. In this exercise, you assign an object to represent each thought you have. Pick something that will be easy for you to move around. It could be dice, a pen, or pebbles. Pick a pebble for every thought you have and move them around for each thought that passes through your mind. Count how many thoughts you have had at the end of a minute. Repeat this several times, trying to have fewer thoughts each time. You will find that all thoughts tend to disappear when you watch them consciously.

- Closing your senses

Sit up comfortably or lie on your back. You can tuck your knees next to your chest if that feels better. Cover your sense organs using your fingers. Begin by placing your thumbs in your ears to ensure you hear nothing. Use your index fingers to cover your eyelids and middle fingers on your nose. The next set of fingers goes above your lips. Keep your shoulders relaxed and your elbows down, and take a deep breath. Breathe deeply enough that you hear your breath very loudly in your head. After ten deep breaths, make your breath so quiet that you hardly hear it. Then, begin listening to sounds through your right ear. Notice all the subtle sounds. Stay here for a couple of minutes, and then release your hands.

- Meditation on the sky

Close your eyes and imagine inner peace, joy, and silence as the clear blue sky. In that sky, clouds of thoughts pass by, but whether or not there are clouds, the sky is always blue. The clouds come, and the clouds go. The blue sky remains unchanging. That is how thoughts should pass through your mind. With or without them, there is always inner peace and joy. Emotions come and go, but that inner peace always stays. It exists inside us as it did before the thoughts came. It will remain when the thoughts disappear. When you look inside, do not look at the clouds. Look deeper into the blue sky. Every time you follow your thoughts, turn your attention to that blue sky within and dive into the silence.

MINDFULNESS AND MEDITATION APPS YOU CAN USE

As you learn to be mindful, you can use apps to make the process easier. The following is a list of apps that you can use. Test and experiment with them until you find one that works best for you and your needs:

1. Headspace

Headspace is the perfect app for beginners and teens new to mindfulness. It has a friendly, animated vibe. As one of the earliest mindfulness apps, it boasts over 70 million downloads and is highly rated on app stores, making it the most popular choice for meditation. Founded by Andy Puddicombe, a former British college student turned Tibetan monk turned app developer, Headspace offers guided meditations with his soothing voice. The app collaborates with other meditation experts and even has a Netflix animated show. The free version provides more than enough resources to practice consistently.

2. Calm

Calm offers a wide range of options for a personalized experience. With over 20 audiovisual nature scenes and soothing music choices, it caters to different needs. It provides multi-day courses for specific issues and features Sound Baths, Breathe Bubble for deep breathing, and Sleep Stories for bedtime relaxation. Calm requires a subscription but offers a 7-day free trial.

3. My Life

Designed for teens and young adults, My.Life focuses on improving self-awareness. It offers a detailed check-in to identify emotions and physical feelings, providing personalized mindfulness exercises based on your current state of mind. From meditations to yoga poses and more, it helps you address various emotions and situations.

4. Smiling Mind

Smiling Mind is made by a nonprofit from Australia and offers a free mindfulness program for adolescents and people of all ages. Its meditations, led by reassuring Aussie voices, come in various lengths, making it easy to fit into busy schedules. The app includes guided meditations for specific activities and life situations, such as transitioning to high school. You can track your progress and set reminders for meditation.

5. Insight Timer

Insight Timer provides an authentic meditation experience, allowing you to customize the duration, sounds, and more. It's suitable for you if you are self-motivated because it offers a DIY approach. The app also provides live meditation events, allowing you to join others virtually in real-time. Most of the content is free, but you have to pay for some.

6. Three Good Things

Three Good Things is a free mindfulness app centered around gratitude. It helps you practice positive psychology and gratitude journaling by recording three things you are grateful for daily. The app aims to make gratitude a consistent habit and offers rewards for streaks of recording grateful moments. It's a simple, pressure-free way to focus on the positive and boost well-being.

In this chapter, you have learned how meditation can improve your resilience and make you a better athlete. You know how it helps you to stay focused by helping to manage your emotions, for example. Take a minute to appreciate that. Set a timer on your phone for two minutes, then put it aside. Sit comfortably and focus on your breath. Feel the air seep into your lungs and then back out through your nose. Notice how it makes you feel. Take another deep breath and try to clear your mind. This is meditation. You are already putting into practice the lessons of this book. Keep doing it.

Find a mindfulness practice that works for you and integrate it into your life. Again, consistency is key. 10 minutes of daily practice is enough to start seeing the benefits of greater calm and a better ability to focus in high-pressure moments. Your athletic performance and your life will thank you for it. In the next chapter, we will consider how to visualize. You will learn how to see and experience the future before it happens. It will be helpful to use alongside meditation to improve your athletic performance.

CHAPTER 3
SEE IT; ACHIEVE IT

Have you ever wondered why some people seem to effortlessly turn their dreams into reality while others struggle to progress? This chapter will help you uncover the truth about visualization and its remarkable potential. Too often, we hear about the wonders of visualization and mistakenly believe that simply imagining things will magically bring them into our lives. But here's the reality: visualization is a powerful tool, but it's just a part of the equation. We must connect its power to our vision and values and couple it with strategic action to harness it. That's what you will learn here.

Think of it like this: in the words of Muhammad Ali, champions aren't solely made in gyms, but rather from something deep inside them—a burning desire, an unwavering dream, and a clear vision. Visualization is the key that unlocks this potential, allowing us to show up as the best version of ourselves. But here's the catch: Visualization is not some mystical force; it's rooted in science—the science of how our brains work. When we combine this understanding with our vision and strategic action, it can indeed feel like magic. However, it's not magic at all; it's merely tapping into more of our brain's potential through a structured and practical system.

This chapter will explore how visualization can help us prepare for challenges, build resilience, and achieve our goals. Like how top athletes use visualization to enhance their athletic performance, you will be able to harness this mental technique to turn your dreams into reality.

STRATEGY #2: VISUALIZE YOUR DESIRED OUTCOMES

Visualization is a technique where you imagine the things you want in your life, big and small. It's like daydreaming but with a purpose. When you visualize, you focus on achieving those things and imagine what it would be like if you accomplished your goals. To do visualization, you ideally find a quiet place, close your eyes, and relax your body. Then, you start thinking about what you want to happen in your life. It's like creating a movie where you see yourself succeeding and feeling happy. For example, if you want to win an award at work, you can close your eyes and imagine yourself receiving the award. You might see yourself on stage, hear people cheering for you, and feel the excitement of holding the award in your hands. Visualization is helpful in many ways, including:

- Improved performance

Athletes use visualization to get better at their sport, and you can also use it to improve your performance. By practicing visualization, you train your mind to focus better, making you more productive and delivering higher-quality results.

- Overcome anxiety

Visualization can help you feel more confident if you feel anxious about something. By imagining yourself succeeding and having a positive response, you can reduce your anxiety and perform better.

- Understand yourself better

Life can get busy, and we may not always know what we want. Visualization helps you think about your goals and desires, which can lead to a deeper understanding of yourself. It can help you set clear goals and determine what you want in life.

- Reduce stress

Visualization can be like a mini escape from stress. When you take time to visualize, you calm your mind and give yourself a break from the pressures of life. It can also help you control your thoughts and reactions, reducing stress in challenging situations.

SEEING IT IN YOUR MIND

Many of us use visualization naturally to help us perform better in sports and fitness activities without realizing it's what we are doing. Have you ever watched an expert's technique closely and then tried to picture yourself doing the same thing in your mind? Or have you mentally practiced your performance before actually doing it? It could be imagining how great it will feel to recover from an injury or the excitement of completing an event you've been training hard for.

Visualization is like a special kind of training where you create images in your mind to learn new skills, plan your strategies, improve your technique, recover from injuries, and become mentally stronger for success in sports. Many Olympic athletes often use this technique—it's one of their top mental resilience tools. Studies done with athletes show that a high percentage of them use visualization regularly to improve their performance.

Recent research has shown that visualization works. It helps athletes improve their skills, boost confidence, handle anxiety, and learn new movements more effectively. That's why athletes, coaches, fitness enthusiasts, and fitness professionals agree that visualization is a powerful tool for performing at your best. Visualization boosts your confidence. According to research, athletes who visualize themselves performing successfully build confidence in their abilities. Seeing themselves achieve their goals in their mind's eye reinforces the belief that they can do it in reality too. This boosted confidence can positively affect an athlete's mindset and performance on the field as they approach challenges with self-assurance.

Visualization requires intense concentration, which helps athletes improve their focus. When they imagine their movements, strategies, and game scenarios, they train their minds to concentrate on specific tasks and stay present during the game. This heightened focus allows athletes to block distractions and perform at their best. It acts as a form of mental rehearsal, where athletes can run through different scenarios and strategies in their minds. This practice enables them to create mental blueprints for their actions, so their responses become more automatic and well-executed when they face similar situations during the game.

Visualization can also help prepare for different game scenarios. In sports, unexpected situations and challenges are expected. Visualization allows athletes to prepare for various scenarios, like making split-second decisions, adapting to opponents' moves, or overcoming setbacks. By mentally rehearsing these situations, athletes can build flexibility and resilience, making them better prepared to handle anything that comes their way during the game.

Visualization is a game-changer if you want to excel in your training and competition. It is like a secret weapon to help you squeeze the maximum out of your training sessions. When you close your eyes and see yourself flawlessly executing those moves you've been practicing, you're not just daydreaming. You're training your brain to perfect your techniques even when you're not physically on the field.

Imagine mentally rehearsing your every move, strategizing, and planning like a champ. Visualization can give you that edge, helping you anticipate your opponents' moves and adapt in real-time. It's like having a crystal ball that lets you foresee different scenarios and be ready to handle anything they throw your way. It speeds up your progress on the road to greatness. When you see yourself reaching your goals in your mind's eye, you're programming your brain for success. It's like setting the GPS to your dream destination; your mind becomes your best co-pilot.

We all know that staying motivated along the way can be tricky. Sometimes, we hit those plateaus or face setbacks that make us question our dedication. But for that, too, visualization can help. Your motivation is significantly boosted when you picture yourself triumphing, achieving greatness, and hoisting that trophy. It's like having your cheerleader urging you to keep pushing forward. And hey, let's not forget those times when training isn't possible. Whether you're nursing an injury or life throws you a curveball, visualization keeps you in top form mentally. When you can't physically train, your mind can keep your skills sharp and your confidence soaring high. It's like a mental gym that is always open, ready to help you stay on top of your game. To reap the benefits of visualization, you have to:

- Get clear on your goals

Before using visualization, knowing what you want to achieve as an athlete is essential. Set clear and specific goals for yourself, like improving your speed, mastering a particular skill, or winning a competition. Knowing your objectives will help you focus your visualization efforts.

- Use more than just images

Visualization is not only about imagining pictures in your mind. Engage all your senses to make it more effective. Feel the movements, hear the sounds, and sense the emotions related to your athletic performance. The more vivid your visualizations, the more effective the technique.

- Do it in real-time

Practice visualization in real-time scenarios. Imagine yourself performing on the field or in a game situation. Visualize how you handle different challenges, opponents, and scenarios you might encounter during competitions. This will help you prepare mentally for various situations.

- Practice

Like any skill, visualization requires practice. Dedicate time each day to sit quietly and visualize your athletic performance. The more you practice, the better you'll become at creating detailed mental images and experiencing the sensations associated with your sport. Make visualization a habit. Incorporate visualization into your daily routine. Whether before a training session or just before going to bed, make it a habit to visualize your athletic success regularly. Consistency is critical to making visualization a powerful tool for improving your performance.

Just like any skill in your sport, visualization takes practice to improve. Treat it like a training exercise and practice regularly to improve. Make sure that your practice focuses on quality over quantity. Visualization can be mentally tiring, so start with 5-10 minute sessions of high-quality imagery. Concentrate on creating clear and vivid images in your mind. Make those images as realistic as you can. When you imagine your sport, include important details that make it feel real. Picture the practice or competition venue, the colors, sounds, and crowd cheering. The more realistic, the better the experience. Over time, build up to 20-30 minutes daily, and you will be astounded by the results.

Whenever possible, plan your imagery. Instead of random images popping up in your mind, plan your imagery to match your current needs. For example, imagine yourself performing perfectly in an upcoming game if you struggle with a specific skill or strategy. Or, if distractions bother you, imagine yourself staying relaxed and focused even in their presence. If you get nervous during competitions, visualize yourself performing confidently under pressure. When you get distracted when performing visualizations, gently bring your attention back. You will get better at this with time. Remember, visualization can be a powerful tool to enhance your performance, but it requires practice and focus. Start with short, quality sessions and gradually build it up over time. With consistent effort, you'll see improvements in your athletic performance.

HOW DOES VISUALIZATION WORK?

Throughout history, people have used visualization techniques to pursue various life goals. These techniques involve focusing intensely on events, people, or objects to bring them into consciousness. Some people may view using imagination for real-life outcomes as mystical, but visualization techniques are grounded in established principles of psychology and neuroplasticity.

When you use visualization to stimulate your goals, it can have several beneficial effects, such as:

- Tapping into your creative potential: Visualization activates your subconscious mind, which can lead to the generation of creative ideas for achieving your goals.
- Programming your brain for success: By visualizing the steps and resources necessary to achieve your goals, you train your brain to recognize and prioritize these resources.
- Boosting motivation: Visualization helps build the motivation to follow through with the resources and actions needed to attain your goals.

Interestingly, whether you realize it or not, your brain naturally employs visualization techniques to simulate future experiences. This instinctual process aids in preparing yourself for what lies ahead. However, by becoming conscious of this process, you can actively participate in shaping your future simulations. By using visualization deliberately, you can improve your ability to reach the goals you've set for yourself. It empowers you to take charge of your future and work toward achieving your athletic goals.

Visualization makes clever use of how our brain works. The brain has this fantastic ability to change and adapt, called neuroplasticity. "Neuroplasticity" means the brain can easily mold and shape itself. It can create new neural pathways and networks based on information and sensory experiences. The exciting part is that this new information and stimulation can come from our imagination; it doesn't have to be real. When you visualize something in your mind, there's very little difference in your brain between what you imagine and what you see in the real world. Even your thoughts send similar signals to your brain as actual actions do. So, the effects of visualization can be seen in how you think and feel, and even in your physical body.

Most of the research on visualization focuses on its physical effects because those are easier to measure. However, it doesn't mean the benefits are limited to the body alone. For instance, a study conducted by the Cleveland Clinic Foundation split ordinary people into two groups. One group did physical exercises, while the other group only visualized doing the workouts in their minds. Surprisingly, both groups showed significant improvements. The physical exercise group increased finger strength by 53%, and the visualization group initially improved by 35% and later by 40%, even after the training had ended.

Visualization works so well because the brain doesn't differentiate between real and imagined scenarios. When you visualize something, the brain activates the same neural pathways as during an actual experience. This means practicing and running through scenarios in your head can be nearly as effective as actually doing them. When athletes like Kobe Bryant use visualization techniques, they activate certain brain functions that prepare them for the actual performance. According to Professor Srini Pillay from Harvard Medical School, our brain creates more connections among different regions when we imagine movements. It stimulates areas involved in rehearsing movements, like the forebrain's putamen, which prepares our brain and body for action. Even picturing others in motion warms up our "action brain" and helps us figure out how to coordinate our actions with theirs. Our brain learns our routine movements with time, making them more automatic and precise. A recent study found that positive visualization during strength training helped participants lift 10-15 more pounds than a control group.

Visualization also involves the reticular activating system (RAS), which is like the brain's filter. This system helps sort out important information from the less important, protecting us from overload and focusing our attention. Visualization techniques can prime the RAS to focus on specific things. For example, if you've been searching for a particular car model and suddenly start seeing it everywhere, your RAS was primed to look for it. You can use this function to your advantage in various areas of life. Focusing on what you want and enjoy makes your brain more likely to identify opportunities related to your goals. It's not magic, but training your mind to notice and seize opportunities when they come your way.

Athletes have known about the incredible power of visualization for a long time. Skilled athletes use their imagination to visualize themselves performing at their best during races and competitions. They create mental pictures of running their races in their desired goal times. Research has found that these athletes first imagine every detail of the race as if they were doing it. Then, after practicing this visualization, they can execute their plans effectively during the actual event.

For example, in one study, nationally ranked male gymnasts from Stanford University used visualizations under hypnosis. They could perform complex tricks they had been struggling with for over a year. Visualization helped them eliminate mistakes, improve flexibility, and enhance their strength. Similarly, in another study, young soccer players boosted their confidence by visualizing their moves before games. It helped them feel more prepared and perform better on the field. High jumpers have also benefited from visualization. By picturing themselves clearing the bar, they improved their performance during high jump events.

VISUALIZATION IN ACTION

Imagine you're an Olympic athlete preparing for the games. You want to perform your best and win a medal. How would you use visualization? Many athletes like you have found how visualization can help boost their performance. Lyndon Rush, the Canadian bobsledder, used visualization to stay focused during the long, tough four years of training leading up to the Olympics. He says he would picture the bobsled track while doing everyday tasks, like brushing his teeth or showering. This mental practice helped him feel ready and familiar with the track before the race.

Another athlete who used visualization is Emily Cook. The seasoned American freestyle skier and three-time Olympian used vivid mental rehearsal to keep her skills sharp and her passion alive. She didn't just see herself skiing; she engaged all her senses. Emily recorded herself describing the perfect jump, feeling the wind on her neck, hearing the crowd, and every little detail of the experience. This made her feel fully prepared and confident when it was time to hit the slopes.

Michael Phelps, the most decorated Olympian ever, also used visualization to prepare for his races. His coach, Bob Bowman, had him watch a "mental videotape" of his races every day before bed and in the morning. Phelps would visualize every moment of swimming a perfect race, from the starting blocks to the finish line and even the victory celebration. This mental practice helped Phelps build a winning mindset and make success a habit.

These athletes show us that visualization is a powerful tool. When you imagine yourself performing perfectly, your brain thinks it's happening. It helps your brain and body work together so that when the actual moment comes, you're ready to shine.

THE PLAYBOOK: CRAFTING YOUR VISION

Whether you're a bobsledder like Rush, a skier like Cook, a swimmer like Phelps, or any athlete, you can use visualization to improve your performance. Picture yourself succeeding, feel the excitement, and hear the crowd's cheers. With the power of your mind, you can turn your dreams into reality and achieve greatness in your sport. Here are some visualization techniques that can get you started:

1. Technique to deal with pressure

As an athlete, pressure can be a motivator, pushing you to do your best. However, when it exceeds a certain threshold, it can have the opposite effect, lowering your performance.

Under extreme pressure, you can use visualization to calm your mind and improve your performance. Visualization can change your emotional state from high-stress and tense to confident, relaxed, and calm.

Begin by finding a quiet place where you will not be interrupted or distracted. Get comfortable, seated on the ground or on a chair. Breathe slowly to relax. You can use a deep breathing mindfulness technique at this stage to make your mind more settled. Then, create an image in your mind. Bring yourself into the moment you feel pressure and add as many details as possible to make it real. Once you have that image, create your optimal emotional state. If you make it real enough, your emotions could become intense. Recognize them and replace them with how you wish to feel. See yourself succeeding. See yourself calm, relaxed, and confident. This technique aims to learn to change your emotional state when you are under pressure. The more you practice it, the better you can handle pressure.

2. Technique to help you relax

Getting relaxed is necessary for success, whether you are trying to learn how to handle pressure, deal with performance anxiety, or any other challenges that affect your performance. Most of the time, we imagine that the more excited we get, the better we play, but that is not true, especially when you tend toward anxiety before a game. You need the ability to relax. Relaxing is a skill, and you can develop it. You can perform the following visualization routine to begin developing your relaxation skills.

Begin by retreating to a quiet place away from distractions. Get into a comfortable sitting position and breathe to get yourself relaxed. Take as many deep breaths as needed to get your mind settled. Then, imagine a situation where you feel most at peace and relaxed. The scene does not matter. The important thing is the emotions you feel. You could imagine yourself reading on a beach or walking your dog. Ensure your image is vivid enough to raise the intense emotions you feel when relaxed. Bring that scene to mind before a game, during a sporting event, or when you feel stressed. The more you do it, the better you become at making yourself feel relaxed, even in high-pressure situations.

3. Technique to master a skill

As mentioned earlier, visualization can help you to master a new skill. This technique aims to help you build neural connections within your brain. In the same way with physical training, you can learn to master a skill using mental exercises. Of course, this technique does not replace physical training. It works as an addition, adding a different facet to training to better your skill level. Like the other techniques, start by finding a quiet place away from distractions. Get into a comfortable sitting position and breathe to get yourself relaxed. Take as many breaths as you need to settle your mind.

Once your mind is settled, start creating your scene. For example, if you are a baseball player, visualize yourself hitting off a tee. See yourself hitting in batting practice and then hitting in a game. Make each of these scenarios as detailed as possible so they feel real. Feel the baseball bat in your hands. Feel the crisp connection when the ball meets the bat's sweet spot. See and feel your success each time. You can use this technique for any skill you like. Use it during training, after training, or before training. It is an invaluable way to get extra practice without physically wearing yourself out.

4. Technique for injury recovery

Your confidence takes a hit after an injury or when you are sidelined. You are unable to train. This does not have to be the case, though. You can use visualization to continue training even if you have an injury. Visualization helps you to strengthen your confidence in your body alongside your skills. One of the hardest parts about returning from an injury is trusting that your body is strong enough to handle the sport. Visualization helps you with this. It helps you to start seeing yourself once again performing in full health.

Begin by finding a quiet place away from any distractions. Get into a comfortable sitting position and take a deep breath to relax. Inhale and exhale as many times as needed while focusing on your breath until your mind is settled. Then, create a scene of yourself performing. Use the same technique for skill mastery and go into the details of your training. You can also visualize parts of a game or a complete game you are playing. The goal is to simulate game-like situations in your mind. From there, visualize yourself healed. See your body being free from injury and performing at peak level. Feel happiness and gratitude for being able to go back to the sport you enjoy. This exercise will help to turn a frustrating situation into an opportunity to grow.

Visualization is an incredible tool for athletes. It helps to create neural connections as you visualize yourself performing in ways that enhance your athletic performance and improve your resilience. It can help you handle pressure, learn a new skill, relax, and recover from an injury. Whichever technique you use, you must be comfortable and away from distractions. You must commit to the process and conjure up as many details as possible for the scenarios to be helpful. The more you practice it, the better you will become. The better you become, the more control you will have over future performance. That is the takeaway for this chapter. In the next one, you will learn another aspect of controlling your athletic performance, which has to do with your emotions. You will learn how to maintain composure and perform well under pressure.

CHAPTER 4
KEEP YOUR COOL

No matter how old you are, there are times in life when you want to throw a tantrum. We all feel frustrated when things don't go as we hoped, and it can be tempting to kick, scream, or break stuff like we did when we were toddlers. But, as we grow up, we learn that's not the answer. The pressure to perform can be intense for young athletes in competitive sports. It's not just about having fun and learning the game; a lot more is happening. You may feel pressure from parents or coaches to win, not disappoint teammates and friends, or compete in positions you aren't confident about. You may also be over-scheduled with too many practices, personal training, schoolwork, and trying to maintain a social life, leading to stress and frustration.

You can still experience anxiety and anger during a game, even if you aren't overcommitted or under pressure. Maybe a call doesn't go your way, or you feel you should have been passed the ball more often. Sometimes, you may take personal responsibility for something that went wrong in the game, seeing it as your failure instead of just part of the team play.

This chapter will explore essential strategies to help you keep things in perspective and stay composed under pressure. We'll focus on emotional regulation, a vital skill for improving performance. As Karon Waddell wisely said, we shouldn't let others manipulate our minds, feelings, or emotions, and we mustn't let them control how we see ourselves. By learning practical techniques to control our emotions effectively, we can find balance and control how we react to various situations.

STRATEGY #3: MASTER YOUR EMOTIONS

Emotions play a significant role in sports. Some emotions, like anxiety, nervousness, or fear before a big game, can feel not so great. When athletes get too nervous, it can mess up their performance. Conversely, some emotions feel fantastic, like happiness and the thrill of winning or mastering a new skill. But have you ever wondered what causes these emotions? Emotions pop up when we're in situations that matter to us, like trying out for a team or winning a competition. It's natural to want to do well in these situations, but sometimes, they can stress us out because there's a lot at stake. Negative emotions like anxiety can sneak in when we don't know what to do or lack confidence.

These emotions can have a significant impact on our bodies and minds. Imagine having a big game tomorrow that you want to win. The pressure might make your heart race, your breathing faster, and your stomach fill with butterflies. And it's hard to stop thinking about the game, making it tough to focus on anything else. These emotional experiences can also affect how we behave and perform. Feeling anxious or fearful might mess up your skills, while feeling happy can boost your performance. But it doesn't stop there–emotions can spread to others too. If one person on a team feels good or bad, it can influence the whole team's mood and even impact their performance in a game. So, understanding emotions in sports is essential. Knowing how they affect you can help you handle them better and improve your game. It will help you conquer your inner game.

CONQUERING YOUR INNER GAME

Sometimes, our emotions can become too much to handle. When they get overwhelming, we need to find ways to manage them. And that's where emotional regulation comes in. Emotional regulation is like trying to control or tone down our emotions. We want to influence which emotions we feel, when we feel them, and how we express them to others. Since emotions can affect both our bodies and minds, we have to deal with the physical effects they have on our bodies and also how they mess with our thoughts and feelings. Emotional regulation is finding ways to handle our emotions better so they don't take over our lives.

Being able to control our emotions effectively matters a great deal. Some people seem to be good at it–they have high emotional intelligence and understand their feelings and those of others. It might seem like they're naturally calm, but they experience negative emotions too. They've learned coping strategies that help them handle difficult emotions. Here's the good news–emotional regulation isn't something fixed or unchangeable. It's a skill that can be learned and improved over time. And when you learn how to manage negative emotions, it's a game-changer for your mental and physical well-being.

As you grow up, you are expected to handle your emotions in socially acceptable ways and help you get through life smoothly. When your emotions get out of control, it can cause many problems. There are a bunch of things that can make emotional regulation harder for you. It could be your beliefs about negative emotions or just not having the right skills to handle them. Sometimes, challenging situations can bring out powerful emotions too. Emotional volatility can mess with your relationships. When you can't properly control your anger, you might end up saying hurtful things to the people you care about, pushing them away. And then, you have to spend time fixing the damage you have caused.

Not just that, when we let our emotions run wild, it can hurt us too. Feeling overwhelming sadness can bring us down and cause a lot of pain. And living in constant fear can hold us back from taking risks and experiencing new things. That is why learning how to regulate and keep your emotions in check is essential. It's not always easy, but it's worth it for your well-being and your relationships with others. There are five emotional regulation skills you need to master:

1. Creating space

Emotions hit us like lightning sometimes. One minute we're okay, and the next, we're furious. The first skill you have to learn is to take a pause. Take a deep breath and slow down between the trigger and your reaction. Give yourself that precious moment to respond in a better way.

2. Noticing your emotions

It's crucial to become aware of your emotions. Dr. Judson Brewer suggests being curious about your physical reactions. Check in with yourself–do you feel the tension in your body? Is your heart racing or your stomach upset? These clues can help you understand what emotions you're going through.

3. Labeling your feelings

After noticing your emotions, give them names. Are you feeling angry, sad, disappointed, or resentful? It could be a mix of emotions. Don't hesitate to identify multiple feelings. And dig deeper–why do you feel this way? Naming your emotions will help you process and even share them with others.

4. Accept your emotions

Remember, it's okay to feel emotions. Emotions are a natural part of being human. Instead of beating yourself up for feeling angry or scared, show yourself some kindness and compassion. Give yourself a break–it's okay to feel what you feel.

5. Practicing mindfulness

Being mindful means living in the moment and paying attention to your inner world. Use your senses to notice things around you without judging them. Mindfulness helps you stay calm and avoid negative thoughts, especially during tough emotional times.

When we face stressful situations, how we handle them sets the stage for everything else. Emotional regulation is the thing that helps us stay on track. It means managing our emotions by filtering what we sense, coping well with stress, staying focused, and getting along with others. It's all about being mindful, staying present, and calmly acknowledging our emotions, feelings, and thoughts.

Here's the cool part: good emotional regulation improves our mental resilience. It strengthens your will to bounce back when things get tough. Take a moment to think about how you handle your emotions and behaviors, especially during challenging times. Ask yourself these questions to discover more about your emotional superpowers:

- How do I control my emotions when things get intense?
- What strategies help me cope with stress effectively?
- How can I stay focused on my game and perform my best?
- Do I get along well with my teammates and other people around me?
- Am I mindful of my emotions, thoughts, and surroundings?

These questions will help you understand yourself better and see what gaps you have as you develop emotional regulation. In sports, emotions are a big deal. They can influence every move you make. Let's take a 45-second shift in ice hockey as an example. A player might feel confident, excited, frustrated, guilty, proud, and angry within that short time. That's six different emotions affecting their performance. That's why it's essential for you, as an athlete, to manage your emotions effectively. To be clear, emotional regulation is changing how you feel and how you respond and act because of those emotions. Emotional regulation keeps you calm under pressure, helps you deal with the highs and lows of competition, and helps you perform consistently every time you play.

THE SCIENCE OF RIDING THE WAVE

Scientific research has shown that emotional regulation is crucial in sports performance and mental resilience. In one study, competitive athletes participated in a laboratory-based experiment with different conditions. They completed a 10km cycling time trial while watching an upsetting video. In some conditions, they were instructed to suppress their emotional reactions to the video, while in others, they had no self-regulation instructions. The results showed that when athletes suppressed their emotions, they performed worse in the cycling task. They completed the trial slower, generated lower mean power outputs, and reached a lower maximum heart rate. This suggests that emotional regulation affects exertion, pacing, and sports performance. You perform better when you can manage your emotions better.

Another study examined the relationship between athletes' emotional regulation and goal achievement in competition. The research found that athletes who increased their positive emotions through self-regulation were likelier to achieve their goals during competitions. On the other hand, those who engaged in affect-worsening emotional self-regulation (negative emotions) were less likely to achieve their goals. Besides, receiving interpersonal emotion regulation (support from others) only contributed to goal achievement when emotional self-regulation was lacking. This indicates that emotional regulation is essential for athletes to perform well and achieve their goals in competitive settings.

The studies suggest that emotional regulation may be more prevalent or have a stronger impact during competitions than at other times, such as practices or training. They also point out that interpersonal emotion regulation, which involves seeking support and understanding from others, occurs more frequently outside of competition. These findings highlight the significance of emotional regulation for sports performance and mental resilience. Athletes who can effectively manage their emotions during competitions tend to perform better and achieve their goals. They conclusively show that suppressing emotions can hinder performance.

In a third study, researchers focused on high-level Italian athletes, including goalkeeper roller-skating hockey players and gymnasts. The researchers implemented an individualized multimodal self-regulation program to optimize the athletes' psychosocial states (emotions, bodily symptoms, and psychological preparation) before competitions. The results indicated that this mental training strategy effectively improved precompetitive states and enhanced competition performance. The study also supported the idea of in and out-of-zone emotions and bodily symptoms within the Individual Zones of Optimal Functioning (IZOF) framework.

Another study involving skilled golfers had researchers investigate emotional and motivational regulation during putting performance after a failure. The athletes were asked to perform putting trials, and the researchers analyzed the frontal alpha asymmetry index (an indicator of emotional and motivational regulation) during these trials. The findings revealed that successful putting was associated with a progressive increase in frontal alpha asymmetry, indicating successful emotional and motivational regulation. Unsuccessful performance was linked to a different pattern of frontal alpha asymmetry.

These studies further emphasize the importance of emotional regulation for athletes' performance. Effective emotional regulation techniques can optimize precompetitive states, enhance performance, and help athletes bounce back after failures. They found that a performer's skill in enabling, sustaining, or controlling their emotions determines their self-regulation. This ability to regulate emotions is crucial in maximizing pre-competition states and enhancing performance. Understanding and utilizing emotional regulation strategies can be crucial for athletes to maintain their mental resilience and achieve peak performance.

It is worth noting that the concept of resilience has evolved to encompass a new theoretical meta-model that suggests the presence of a "resilience filter" made up of various biopsychosocial protective factors. These factors act as a shield, helping people cope with challenges and adversities they encounter in life. Emotional regulation has been named as one of those protective factors.

For athletes, emotional regulation becomes a crucial aspect of their resilience toolkit. Sports can be highly physically and mentally demanding, and athletes often face various stressors and pressures, both on and off the field. By possessing strong emotional regulation skills, athletes can navigate the ups and downs of sports with more ease and composure. When faced with setbacks, failures, or high-pressure situations, emotional regulation helps athletes maintain focus, stay motivated, and recover quickly from setbacks. It allows them to bounce back from challenges, adapt to new situations, and perform at their best consistently.

Furthermore, emotional regulation also fosters positive relationships and effective communication with coaches, teammates, and other individuals involved in sports. By expressing emotions in a controlled manner and understanding the emotions of others, athletes can foster a supportive and cohesive team environment. Emotional regulation empowers you to withstand the demands and stressors of sports, enhances your mental and emotional well-being, and contributes to your overall performance and success in sports.

Emotions can either sharpen or distract focus, depending on how they are managed. Athletes with strong emotional regulation skills can focus on their task, filtering out distractions and negative thoughts. They can stay emotionally composed, which helps them better concentrate on the game plan, read opponents' movements, and make split-second decisions.

Under pressure, emotions can lead to impulsive or irrational decisions, but athletes who effectively manage their emotions are less likely to make hasty choices. Instead, they can maintain a clear and rational mindset, enabling them to make well-calculated decisions even in tense situations. This skill becomes particularly crucial in critical moments of a game or match.

In high-pressure situations that often trigger intense emotions, such as anxiety or nervousness, athletes with strong emotional regulation skills can keep these emotions in check, preventing them from becoming overwhelming. This ability allows them to perform at their best, even when the stakes are high. They can access their skills and techniques more efficiently, execute game plans with composure, and avoid choking under pressure. Eventually, this translates to a longer and better career. Athletes who can manage their emotions are better equipped to handle the ups and downs of their careers, including injuries, losses, and setbacks. They are more resilient and can bounce back from disappointments with greater ease. This resilience helps them sustain their motivation and passion for the sport. It promotes mental well-being, reducing the risk of burnout.

EMOTIONAL REGULATION IN ACTION

Roger Federer's journey from a hot-headed athlete to one of the industry's calmest and most composed players is a remarkable transformation that reflects his growth as a person and as a tennis legend and the power of emotional regulation. In his early career days, Federer was known for his fiery temper on the court. He often expressed frustration and anger when things didn't go his way, smashing rackets and engaging in heated arguments with officials. While his talent and skills were undeniable, his emotional outbursts occasionally hindered his performance and led to missed opportunities.

As Federer matured and gained more experience in the tennis world, he recognized the need to change his approach. He understood that emotional regulation was crucial for maintaining focus and consistency in his game. Federer dedicated the next couple of years to working on his mindset and finding a balance between his fiery, competitive spirit and calm composure. He described it as having the "fire and desire to win" while also maintaining the "ice coolness" to handle losses and mistakes gracefully. Achieving this mental progress wasn't easy for Federer, and he sought help from a psychologist to address his anger issues in 1998 and 1999.

During this time, Federer's former coach, Paul Dorochenko, revealed that they enlisted the support of a sports psychologist who worked closely with Federer from his late teens to early twenties. This collaboration with the sports psychologist played a significant role in stabilizing Federer's mental game and setting him on the path to a triumphant career. Though Federer has not extensively spoken about the specifics of his mental work, the impact is evident in his transformation from a hot-headed athlete to one of tennis's most composed and successful players. This journey exemplifies the importance of addressing and managing one's emotions to reach the peak of athletic performance and personal growth.

In time, the transformation was evident on the court. Federer became renowned for his calm and collected demeanor, regardless of the match's intensity or importance. He showed grace under pressure, responding to challenges with poise and confidence. This newfound emotional control translated into improved decision-making, focus, and performance, elevating his game to new heights. It laid the foundation for his golden era of Grand Slam dominance, starting at Wimbledon in 2003. Off the court, Federer's transformation was equally impressive. He became known for his sportsmanship and humility, earning the respect and admiration of fans, fellow players, and the tennis community. He embodied the true spirit of a champion, not only through his exceptional skills but also through his demeanor and behavior.

Roger Federer is one of the greatest tennis players in history for his incredible achievements on the court and his journey of self-improvement and emotional growth. His story is a powerful reminder of the importance of emotional regulation in sports and life, inspiring athletes worldwide to embrace this aspect of their development for long-term success and fulfillment.

THE PLAYBOOK: STRATEGIES FOR WINNING THE MENTAL GAME

1. Progressive Muscle Relaxation (PMR)

This technique involves a two-step process of tensing and then relaxing muscle groups to promote a sense of calmness and composure. It allows you to give your emotional energy somewhere by channeling it outside the body to manage your emotions effectively and navigate challenging situations. Our bodies typically react physically to anger, frustration, or worry. You may notice signs like a racing heart, tight muscles, or a funny feeling in the stomach. These signs help you know how you are feeling.

Studies have shown that this technique has numerous health benefits. It reduces anxiety and tension, making it practical for people with generalized anxiety disorders or stress. PMR has been found to improve sleep quality, making it a helpful tool for those experiencing sleep difficulties due to anxiety or physical conditions. PMR has also shown promising results in alleviating pain in various body areas. It has been found to ease neck pain, reduce low back pain, and even decrease the frequency of migraine episodes. PMR has effectively improved systolic blood pressure for people with hypertension. The technique also benefits individuals experiencing temporomandibular joint (TMJ) disorder, which causes stiffness and pain in the jaw due to emotional stress.

PMR is simple to do at home. All you need is a quiet space without distractions and some focus. The idea is to tense each muscle group and hold for 5 seconds. Then, you fully relax those muscles for 10 seconds before moving on to the next muscle group. Begin sitting or lying down with your body relaxed. Take five deep and slow breaths. Lift your toes upward, hold for five seconds, and then let go. Pull them downward, hold them for five seconds, and let go. Repeat the same tense and relax sequence for your calf muscles, knees, thigh muscles, buttocks, hands, arms, abdominal muscles, chest, shoulders, lips, mouth, and eyes.

Doing PMR for the first time when upset is not a good idea. Begin by practicing it when you are calm. The more you practice, the easier it will be to use PMR when you need to calm yourself down. There is no wrong or right way to relax your muscles as long as you do it. You can even change the order in which you relax your muscle groups. Find a way that works for you.

   2. Cue words

In-game situations, you might notice players who make a mistake reacting by stomping the ground, muttering to themselves, and displaying frustration. While it might seem like a way to let off steam (better than throwing a punch), it's not productive. Here's why you need to handle such situations differently.

You lose focus on the game when you are busy beating yourself up. You might miss defensive opportunities, fail to chase rebounds, or overlook flaws in your opponents' strategies. This self-criticism also puts extra pressure on you with negative self-talk like, "I must do better" or "Don't mess up again." Besides, getting angry with other players may lead to conflicts with officials or upset fans. As an athlete, your goal is to get back into the game immediately after a mistake. One effective way to do this is to use positive word cues.

You can use phrases like "Next Time," "Nice Try," "Get Back," or "Rebound." These cues are positive motivators that instantly redirect your focus to the game. In cases where the mistake triggers genuine anger, these cue words can help channel that energy into working even harder to overcome challenges. Cue words are powerful tools that can help you with focus, motivation, and instruction. They are unique to each athlete and can be placed in various locations, such as your locker, equipment, or bedroom wall.

The purpose of a cue word is to help you re-center during games and bounce back from frustration, adversity, and failure. For instance, you might choose a word like "State" as a reminder of your ultimate goal and write it on your palm before every competition. Acronyms can also be effective, like "FOEP" for "Focus on Every Play" or "RMFP" for "Reach My Full Potential."

Athletes use cue words because emotions in competition can easily distract from success. Take, for example, a baseball/softball player who strikes out; negative emotions might overwhelm them, causing them to forget that it's just one at bat and that more opportunities await. A cue word can swiftly redirect your focus, energy, and enthusiasm toward the next chance for success.

You can make your cue words to keep you calm during the game. As you do, keep these tips in mind:

- Make the word your own and ensure it holds personal meaning. No word, phrase, or acronym is too silly if it resonates with you.
- Avoid making the cue words overly long or confusing. The goal is to recall it quickly during games so you can promptly refocus on success.
- Place your cue word where you'll see it—remember, it's pointless if you can't remember it during competition.

- Try to use your cue word before each play. For instance, if you play football, think of your cue word moments before each snap to shift your attention to a positive thought.

3. Emotional journaling

Imagine a business setting its budget for the year and waiting to see what happens after 12 months. That wouldn't work. Businesses regularly review their finances, adjust expenses, and adapt their goals according to the financial climate. Similarly, regular reflection helps athletes evaluate their training, determine what works and doesn't, and make changes to improve their performance. This is where emotional journaling comes in.

Keeping a journal unlocks knowledge and energy to help athletes break plateaus and become faster, stronger, and more skilled. Journaling allows you to honestly and accurately review your past experiences. This not only helps you learn about effective training strategies but also helps you learn more about yourself. A journal can help you find the best times for you to train. It would boost your motivation and increase confidence as you reflect on your past performance. It also improves your focus and keeps you from being sidetracked.

Most importantly, an emotional journal will keep you self-aware. It enhances self-monitoring and emotional regulation by serving as a reference tool. You also get a non-judgmental outlet for venting your frustrations and celebrating your achievements, especially when friends and family may not fully understand the pressures of being an athlete. There are many types of journaling that you can try, but here are three to get you started:

- Gratitude journaling

Each day, list three or more aspects you feel grateful for. This simple act has a powerful impact on relieving stress. It shifts your focus to the positive resources in your life and creates a more positive mood. These benefits have been shown to build long-term resilience. Your journal will become a record of all the beautiful moments that have enriched your days so that if you ever feel down in the future, you can turn to those pages and remind yourself of the many things you have to appreciate in your sporting life.

- Emotional release journaling

You can also use your journal to express your emotional responses to the day's events. That way, it becomes a way to cope with stress and process your feelings. Record the different significant events of the day and how you responded to them. Once that's done, you can explore positive reframing options for the negative responses.

- Self-reflection journaling

In this case, you take a moment to consider what you've learned in the past 24 hours that can move you closer to your desired destination. Are there situations where you could have acted differently for a better outcome? This journaling practice provides an opportunity for self-reflection, learning, and letting go of things holding you back.

No matter the journaling practice you choose, stay consistent. Decide whether you like pen and paper or a digital platform for journaling, and stick with your chosen medium. Be sure to create a routine. Set aside dedicated time each day for journaling. Consistency is key whether it's in the morning, evening, or integrated into your sports ritual. Select a specific theme for your journaling, and be honest and vulnerable. Write authentically, without judgment, expressing your thoughts, emotions, and experiences. Journaling can be useful in your journey toward well-being, growth, and self-improvement. Embrace the process and watch its positive impact on your emotional regulation.

To bring it closer home, take a piece of paper and set it aside for at least three minutes. Think about the contents of this chapter. How well do you understand emotional regulation? Have you identified gaps in the way you manage your emotions? In those heated moments during a game, can you keep your cool? Journal about this. This is an example of self-reflection journaling. You have practiced something you have learned already, and that's a big step toward victory. In the next chapter, you will discover how to set goals, define what victory looks like for you, and track your progress toward it like a pro.

CHAPTER 5
DESTINATION: VICTORY

Many young athletes have goals about what they aim for in competition but do not have well-defined goals for practice and training. Training is necessary if you will succeed in competition; the best athletes are athletes who train smart. They have well-defined goals for their practice sessions and their sporting activities. In this chapter, you will learn to be one of the best. You will learn how to imagine success in your dreams, want it in your heart, and, in the words of Joe Montana, expect it to come true because there is no other way to do it. This chapter will teach you why goal setting matters, how to set achievable goals, and how to effectively monitor your progress toward them.

STRATEGY #4: SET STRATEGIC GOALS

You might have heard about goal setting, described as choosing and labeling a target you want to achieve. But there's a more helpful perspective we should consider. Instead of just thinking about what success looks like for you, let's start with a different question: What kind of pain are you willing to endure? This is a strategy the author Mark Manson teaches. He realized that setting a goal is the easy part. Who wouldn't want to achieve something great, like writing a best-selling book or getting in shape? We all want that.

The real challenge lies in deciding if you're ready to make the sacrifices required to achieve your goal. Are you genuinely willing to embrace the lifestyle that comes with it, including the less glamorous parts? It's easy to dream big, but facing the trade-offs that come with our aspirations is harder. We all want the gold medal, but not everyone wants to train like an Olympian.

Here's a key insight from Mark Manson–goal setting is not just about choosing the rewards you want, but also understanding and accepting the costs involved. Think of your goals as the rudder of a small rowboat. They steer you in a particular direction and determine where you're headed. If you stick to one goal, the rudder stays steady, and you make progress. But if you keep changing your goals, it's like constantly moving the rudder around, and you might find yourself going in circles.

Now, there's something even more critical than the rudder–the oars. If the rudder is your goal, the oars represent your achievement process. While the rudder sets your course, the oars propel you forward. This rudder and oars metaphor helps us distinguish between systems and goals, and it's an important distinction that applies to all aspects of life. As an athlete, your goal might be running a marathon or winning a basketball tournament, and your system is your training schedule for the month.

Goals give you direction, while systems drive your progress. The real benefit of having a goal is that it guides you in creating the right system to achieve it. But remember, you can't just hold onto the rudder and expect to get somewhere; you have to row with those oars. Goal setting is creating a destination and effective systems to get you there. Setting goals is like creating a roadmap for your journey toward achieving specific results in the future. It's not just about wishful thinking; it involves setting practical and realistic targets to strengthen your commitment to the rules and consistently improve your nutrition, training, and daily habits, such as sleep.

In sports, goal setting plays a crucial role for athletes. It's a powerful psychological technique that instills motivation and helps you focus on individual aspects of your training, nutrition, and lifestyle to address weaknesses and improve. Each goal is a stepping stone toward your long-term aspirations, making success more attainable with focused and achievable targets. Research and studies have proven that setting strategic goals in sports leads to better performance. It boosts morale, motivation, and dedication, translating into commitment and persistence. Goals provide the much-needed focus, maintain high motivation, and bring positive changes in progress, direction, and overall satisfaction when achieved.

When setting goals in sports, it's essential to follow a goal-setting approach that makes them achievable. The goals you focus on should be personally meaningful to you, as this will maintain your motivation and increase your likelihood of success. While coaches may set some training goals to enhance performance and personal development, you must agree with and value these goals. They should challenge you to become a better athlete and align with your aspirations. Remember, you don't have to tackle your goals alone, especially as an athlete. Seek help and support when needed. Professionals in various sports science fields can be valuable resources to consult. Additionally, your friends and family can provide vital support during tough times, like injury setbacks or unexpected defeats, helping you stay resilient and focused on continuous improvement. As you set your goals, here are three strategies to help you follow through:

- Eliminate your goals ruthlessly

Imagine your goals are competing for your time and attention, just like burners on a stove. When you focus on one goal, the others might suffer. The good news is that progress comes faster by pausing less critical things and dedicating yourself to one goal at a time. Don't fall for the idea that you need bigger goals. Instead, choose wisely and eliminate distractions. Like pruning a rose bush, cutting away some goals allows the remaining ones to blossom fully. Do away with the less important goals and keep only those you most resonate with.

- Stack your goals

Research shows that making specific plans for when, where, and how you'll work on your goals increases your chances of success. It's called "implementation intentions." One clever way to use this is through habit stacking. Just fill in the blanks:

"After/before [current habit], I will [new habit]."

For instance, you can stack meditation with your morning coffee or push-ups before your morning shower. This technique links your new goals to existing daily habits, making it easier to follow through. Creating specific plans and triggers bridges the gap between your goals and the daily process of achieving them.

- Set an upper limit

Usually, we focus on the minimum threshold we want to achieve, like "I want to lose at least 5 pounds this month." It's like aiming for the minimum and thinking, "If I can do more, great!"

But what if we added an upper limit to our goals and behaviors? For example: "I want to lose at least 5 pounds this month, but not more than 10."

Setting an upper limit creates a magical zone for long-term growth. It's about pushing hard enough to progress without going overboard and burning out. Having an upper limit helps you sustain your progress and stay consistent. This is especially important when you're starting on a new goal. The top priority is showing up regularly. Even more than immediate success, forming the habit of showing up sets the foundation for future improvement. If you don't show up consistently, you won't have anything to build on and grow in the future.

WHY GOALS MATTER

We have already established that resilience is a defining trait for athletes, enabling them to bounce back from challenges, setbacks, and adversities with determination and strength. Goal setting is a powerful tool to enhance resilience. When athletes set clear, specific, and achievable goals, they lay the foundation for building their mental toughness and overcoming obstacles. Setting clear and specific goals acts as a roadmap for you, guiding you toward your desired outcomes. When you have a well-defined destination, you gain a sense of direction and purpose in your pursuits. This clarity of purpose allows you to stay focused on what you want to achieve, even amidst the chaos and uncertainties of the athletic journey. Having a roadmap makes you less likely to get lost or derailed by distractions, enabling you to stay on course and work toward your objectives with steadfast determination.

The mere act of setting goals ignites motivation within athletes. Specific and achievable goals provide you with something tangible to strive for, creating an intrinsic drive to put in the effort required to achieve them. Goals constantly remind you of the rewards waiting at the finish line, fueling your determination to persevere through challenging times. When you see the direct link between your efforts and attaining your goals, your motivation skyrockets, and you become more willing to endure temporary discomfort for long-term gain.

As we progress toward our goals, we experience a boost in self-confidence. The achievement of smaller milestones validates our abilities and reinforces our belief in our capacity to succeed. This growing sense of confidence becomes an essential asset when facing adversity. When we encounter challenges, we can draw upon our past successes to bolster our confidence and maintain a positive outlook, ultimately making us more resilient in the face of difficulties.

Goal setting is a potent catalyst for improving our resilience. By setting clear, specific, and achievable goals, we find direction, motivation, and confidence to pursue our dreams relentlessly. It creates a robust foundation for us to cultivate our resilience, enabling us to navigate the highs and lows of our athletic journey with unwavering determination and strength. Goal-setting is not just a pathway to success but a cornerstone of mental fortitude.

As it turns out, there are principles for effective goal setting. The goals need to be specific, measurable, and observable. You need to be clear and specific about what you want to achieve. Avoid general statements like "improve shooting percentage in basketball." Instead, set specific criteria and directives like "draw a 'C' with your wrist and use the cue word 'push' to improve shooting mechanics." Measurable goals allow you to quantify your progress. Make sure the goal has a timeline to work toward. Specify whether the goal will be accomplished by the end of practice, week, or playoffs. Timely goals create urgency and help athletes focus on their efforts within a defined timeframe.

Effective goals are moderately challenging. Opt for moderately challenging goals rather than setting easy or overly difficult ones. Moderate goals push athletes to work harder and extend themselves, fostering a sense of accomplishment and satisfaction when achieved. Write them down in detail and keep a journal or a publicly posted goal monitoring chart to stay accountable. As a rule of thumb, ensure your goals are short- and long-range. Goal-setting is like climbing a mountain. Utilize short-term goals strategically to progress toward your long-term objectives.

While at it, set practice as well as competition goals. Acknowledge the importance of effective practices in preparing for competitions. Practice goals should align with competition performance goals and focus on work ethic, attitude, mental skills, and team cohesion. Ensure that you internalize each one of your goals. It will help you keep going even when things get tough.

THE SCIENCE BEHIND GOAL SETTING

Research has shown that setting goals can restructure your brain to make it more effective in achieving what you desire. Your brain's emotional center (the amygdala) evaluates how important the goal is to you. Your problem-solving area (the frontal lobe) defines the specifics of the goal, and then the two work together to keep you focused on actions that lead to your goal and avoid distractions. This brain process is like a computer program but is more complex because your brain has neuroplasticity. Setting goals can literally change your brain's structure to optimize achieving them.

Researchers found that setting ambitious goals can even help heal brains. For example, people with multiple sclerosis who set wellness goals had fewer and less severe symptoms. Highly emotional goals (ones you really want to achieve) make obstacles seem less significant. Ambitious goals also motivate your brain more than easy ones. Studies showed that people committed to challenging goals performed better and saved more energy than those with easy goals. So, if you want your brain to work at its best, set specific and challenging goals. They direct attention, increase effort, boost persistence, and motivate you to develop better strategies.

GOAL-SETTING IN ACTION

It is one thing to read the science, but it makes it even more impactful when you see other people who have applied it and succeeded. Here, you'll find the stories of three such athletes. These inspiring athletes have proven that effective goal-setting and progress tracking can be instrumental in achieving greatness. Their unwavering focus, dedication, and commitment to improvement have led to extraordinary individual success and inspired countless athletes worldwide to follow in their footsteps.

As a boy, Michael Phelps discovered his love for swimming. From an early age, he was a goal-oriented athlete, guided by his long-time coach, Bob Bowman. At just 8 years old, Michael crafted a goal sheet that revealed his dream of making it to the Olympics. What stood out about his goals was their clarity and the presence of a detailed plan of action. Michael understood that merely setting a goal was insufficient; he needed a vehicle for change. He knew that to achieve his dreams, he had to work hard and attend every practice, which he did with unwavering dedication.

As he blossomed, he honed his goal-setting skills further. In the run-up to the 2008 Beijing Olympics, he set specific targets for each of his events. Even amid unexpected challenges, like swimming blind due to leaky goggles in the 200-

meter butterfly, Michael came remarkably close to his goal time. His goal was to swim 1:51.1, and he achieved a breathtaking 1:51.5, showcasing his ambition and yet realistic approach to setting goals. Michael proved the power of setting and striving for specific goals with each stroke. His incredible achievements include an astounding 22 Olympic medals, world records in various relays and disciplines, and more international medals than most developed countries.

Like Michael Phelps, Usain Bolt, the iconic six-time Olympic Games gold medallist, is an excellent example of what goal setting can do for athletes. With his lightning speed and charismatic personality, Bolt has captivated the world and left a lasting impact on track and field. At the launch of his autobiography in London, Bolt shared a valuable insight into his success–the importance of setting goals in life. He believes that setting clear and meaningful goals is the key if one aspires to be the best or aims to achieve greatness.

Throughout his illustrious career, Bolt consistently set ambitious targets for himself. From the early days of his training to the grand stages of the Olympic Games, he had a vision of what he wanted to achieve. Having his sights firmly set on specific goals, he could channel his energy and focus into training and competitions. Bolt's goal-setting approach went beyond just dreaming big; he backed it up with hard work. He knew that setting goals was only the first step, and his dedication and effort to realize those goals made all the difference. Bolt's incredible achievements on the track speak for themselves. He is the fastest man on the planet. His commitment to goal-setting and natural talent transformed him into a sporting legend.

There are many examples of athletes who embody goal-setting in their careers, but the last one of note is Serena Williams. In one press conference, the tennis legend revealed her unwavering commitment to setting and pursuing her goals. The 23-time Grand Slam winner said that one of her top goals was maintaining her health. Staying fit and injury-free was a constant goal for her, enabling her to continue competing at the sport's highest level. But her ambitions went far beyond merely staying healthy. Serena's main focus was excelling in tournaments and aiming to keep the coveted No. 1 ranking worldwide.

For Serena, tournaments served as milestones that marked her progress and achievements. She was motivated by the challenge of performing at her best on the grandest stages of tennis. The desire to stay on top of the rankings fueled her determination and spurred her to achieve greatness. She started playing tennis with the simple goal of enjoying the sport and winning tournaments. As she continued to compete and grow as an athlete, her aspirations expanded, and she began to embrace the numbers and achievements that came with her success. Serena Williams is a shining example of how goal-setting and a relentless pursuit of excellence can lead to a legendary career. Her dedication to her craft, hunger for success, and genuine love for the game made her one of the greatest athletes ever.

THE PLAYBOOK: SETTING GOALS AND TRACKING PROGRESS

1. Set different types of goals

You should set three types of goals to boost your performance and achieve success in your sport. Firstly, you can set process goals. Process goals are about the steps and actions needed to improve your skills. Think of them as the building blocks of your progress. For example, if you're a basketball player, a process goal could be to practice shooting free throws for 30 minutes daily. These goals help you focus on the specific things you must do daily to improve.

Secondly, you can set performance goals. These goals are all about measuring your progress and achievements. They allow you to see how well you're doing and if you're on track with your development. Performance goals could be hitting specific points in a game or improving your sprint time. They help you gauge your improvement and motivate you to keep pushing harder. Lastly, set outcome goals. These are the big dreams, the ultimate results you want to achieve. They are the championships you want to win, the records you want to break, or the top rankings you aspire to reach. Outcome goals are exciting and give you something to aim for, but remember, they depend on many factors, so it's essential to have process and performance goals along the way.

To maximize your success, using all three types of goals is crucial. Process goals keep you grounded in the day-to-day work, performance goals let you track your progress, and outcome goals inspire you with big dreams. So, set a mix of these goals, create a plan, and stay committed to working hard.

2. Set your goals when it counts most

Goal setting is an excellent tool that you can use anytime you want to improve and achieve greatness. But there are some specific occasions when it can be super helpful. Before the start of a new season is a perfect time to set goals. You can work with your coaches and teammates to determine what you want to achieve individually and as a team. These pre-season goals will help you focus on areas where you want to improve and bring the whole team together around common objectives.

Secondly, goal setting becomes supercritical when you're dealing with injuries. Setting goals is a fantastic way to stay motivated if you ever get hurt and need rehabilitation. Work closely with your athletic trainer to set small and big milestones for your recovery. This will help you track your progress and keep your eyes on the prize of returning to full strength.

Remember that they should be meaningful to you, no matter when or why you set goals. If you feel a strong connection to and take ownership of your goals, you'll be more committed to achieving them.

3. Set effective goals

The SMART framework is your best friend for setting effective goals. SMART is an acronym for Specific, Measurable,

Attainable, Realistic, and Time-bound goals. Your goals should be crystal clear and super specific. Avoid vague goals like "get better at basketball." Instead, be specific, like "improve my three-point shooting accuracy by 10%." Make sure you can measure your progress. Use numbers or other ways to track your improvements. This way, you'll know exactly how close you are to achieving your goal.

Your goals should also be challenging but realistic. Goals that are too easy won't push you, and goals that are too far-fetched might discourage you. Find that sweet spot where it's a stretch but doable. Make sure your goals are meaningful and relevant to what you want to achieve. Think about how they fit into your overall plan and what you want to accomplish, then give yourself a deadline. Set a specific time frame to achieve your goals. This will help you stay focused and motivated.

Here's the cool thing: goals are not set in stone. Life happens, and sometimes, you need to adjust your goals along the way. Don't worry if you don't achieve a particular goal right away. It doesn't mean you failed. It means you have reached a 'checkpoint.' A checkpoint lets you see how you're doing and helps you make any necessary adjustments. Remember, it's all about progress, not perfection.

4. Set your goals fast (15 minutes)

In only 15 minutes, you can follow the following steps to set goals that work for you:

Step 1: Figure out what you want to accomplish. Think about what you want to achieve. Don't hold back, even if your goals seem big or crazy. Having a precise aim is essential, and this is your outcome goal. Grab a pencil or pen and write your goal down.

Step 2: Find out why you want it. Next, ask yourself why you want to go after this goal. This will give you more motivation and help you stay determined. Use a pencil to write the answer to this question next to your goal. List all the reasons why you're excited to reach your goal.

Step 3: What will you do? Now, think about the actions you'll take to achieve your goal. This part is called action steps. Write this question in pencil and list your actions as they come to you using a green marker pen.

Step 4: What will hinder you? It's important to identify obstacles that might get in your way. This step teaches you to recognize and avoid counter-productive actions. List the obstacles that you envision next with a red marker pen.

Step 5: Commit to your goals. Once you are done with step 4, write this statement at the bottom of your paper: "Everything in green works for me. Everything in red will not help me. My day should be filled with items marked in green. My day should not be filled with red items." Then, use a green marker to sign your sheet.

Step 6: Place your goals strategically. The last step is simple–tape your goal chart to a wall you see daily. Seeing your goals regularly will remind you to stay disciplined and keep working toward them.

When asked to provide some tips for goal setting, Michael Phelps advised athletes to put their goals somewhere prominent. You will notice that that's the spirit of the sixth step in the goal-setting process. From him, we also learn why it matters to write down your goals. Just dreaming about them won't cut it. Writing it down makes your goal real, more than just wishful thinking. Your brain gets to work, figuring out how to make it happen. And here's some proof that writing down your goal matters: a study found that people were 42% more likely to stick to their goals when they wrote them down.

Once you have set your goals, remember to team up with your coach. Your coach can't read your mind, so talk to them about your goals. Share what you think it takes to achieve them and get their feedback. If you need extra help in a specific area, ask for it. Having your coach on board adds another layer of accountability, especially on tough training days. Phelps had a no-nonsense coach, Bowman, who kept him focused when motivation wavered. Your coach doesn't have to be the same, but a strong partnership can lead to greatness, and when setbacks happen, bounce back. Even champions like Phelps dealt with setbacks. He had his share of disappointments and obstacles but never gave up. In the next chapter, you will learn about the mindset that kept him going instead of giving up. You will understand how to cultivate a growth mindset.

CHAPTER 6
THE CHAMPION'S MIND

What if I told you that in sports and life, the actual battle lies not on the field but within the confines of your mind? We often face challenges, setbacks, and obstacles that make us feel stuck or defeated. But, the most significant obstacle is not the external forces at play but our own beliefs and attitudes–our mindset. A mindset consists of your beliefs and everything that shapes how you see yourself, the people around you, and the world. It is your mindset that influences the way you feel, think, and act in any particular situation.

Since we all have different backgrounds, upbringings, and cultures, we also develop different mindsets depending on our situations. Those mindsets can be divided into two–a growth mindset and a fixed mindset. This chapter looks into the transformative power of cultivating a growth mindset—a key strategy to fortify our mental resilience and elevate athletic performance. A growth mindset is an antidote to unleash your hidden potential and propel you toward athletic greatness.

Here, you will discover how your mindset shapes your perspective, influences your actions, and ultimately determines your outcomes. You will be equipped with practical, actionable steps to cultivate and nourish a growth mindset. By understanding the power of this mindset, you will gain the tools to approach challenges enthusiastically, learn from failures with grace, and continuously evolve into a stronger, more capable version of yourself.

STRATEGY #5: CULTIVATE A GROWTH MINDSET

A growth mindset involves believing you can develop your skills and abilities through hard work, the proper strategies, and guidance from others. It's a powerful idea coined by Professor Carol Dweck in her book, "Mindset: The New Psychology of Success." Professor Dweck's research shows that those who believe in their ability to grow and improve tend to achieve more than those who think their talents are fixed and unchangeable. People with a growth mindset see opportunities where others see obstacles, always challenging themselves to learn and grow beyond their comfort zone.

The cool thing is we can all cultivate a growth mindset. Each of us has the potential to develop this way of thinking. Knowing this fact is already a big step in the right direction. You have a fixed mindset if you do not have a growth mindset. A fixed mindset is when people believe their abilities are fixed from birth and can't be changed much. It's thinking you're stuck with what you've got and there's little room for improvement. But here's the thing, a fixed mindset can be limiting in many situations. People with a fixed mindset often focus on showing off their strengths and avoiding situations that might reveal their weaknesses. As a result, they miss out on valuable opportunities to learn and grow.

The key to success in any aspect of life is embracing a growth mindset. It's all about believing that your abilities can be developed through effort and experience. With a growth mindset, you're ready to take on challenges, learn from setbacks, and keep pushing yourself to new heights. In academia, some studies suggest that how well you perform academically can influence your mindset and vice versa. It's like a positive feedback loop. Researchers found that even a short online growth mindset course can help boost student performance. Once students learn that they can develop their intellectual abilities through effort and learning, they try harder in class. Researchers wanted to determine how this intervention affected math performance and enrolment in secondary education in the US.

Even so, researchers do not fully agree on this. A different study from the University of Edinburgh showed no clear benefit in growth mindset theory for students aged nine to thirteen. Others argue that factors like intelligence and personality play a more significant role in predicting success at school and work. These traits tend to be more stable, especially in adults.

Conversely, more recent research by Dr. Dweck and the OECD (Organization for Economic Cooperation and Development) has shown some positive outcomes. In 2021, data revealed that schools can encourage a growth mindset by rewarding progress, trying different learning strategies, and providing meaningful feedback. In one of the studies, students were asked how much they believed their intelligence was fixed and unchangeable. Those who disagreed (meaning they had a growth mindset) scored higher in reading, science, and math than those who agreed (fixed mindset). There's still more to learn about growth mindsets and how they impact academic learning. Researchers overwhelmingly agree, though, on the impact of a growth mindset on athletic performance.

Athletes with a fixed mindset believe that they should avoid challenges. They believe you either have the skills and abilities to navigate them or you don't. They figure there is no point in persevering because their skills will not improve. They may work hard only when convinced they have the skill they are working on, not because they are trying to improve. And when they receive feedback, they take it personally like they take failure. Because of these beliefs, these athletes tend to get emotional and fall into the comparison trap. They are often rigid and fearful.

Athletes with a growth mindset believe that people can improve their abilities and skills. They trust their hard work will improve their abilities and see challenges as a chance to test their mettle. They know that effort will eventually yield mastery, and feedback is a learning tool in that process. They do not take feedback or failure personally. Athletes with this mindset win and lose gracefully and enjoy other people's successes. Their mindset makes them open-minded, calm, coachable, and hard-working.

In which of these two categories do you fall?

Amazingly, you can develop the two types of mindsets anytime, anywhere, and in any situation. Your brain functions and thinking patterns can change, and that's pretty cool. But when it comes to choosing between a growth mindset and a fixed mindset, the ideal one to go for in any situation is a growth mindset. As an athlete, a growth mindset will make you a lifelong learner. Athletes with a growth mindset are always open to learning more. They appreciate lifelong learning and constantly seek new skills, techniques, and knowledge to improve their sports performance. They have an insatiable hunger for growth. It will guarantee you career growth and success. If you are constantly developing, you are willing to improve and embrace new challenges, which pave the way for your career to flourish. Conversely, a fixed mindset can hold you back and hinder progress.

A growth mindset not only impacts your performance but also boosts your self-esteem. When you believe you can continually improve, failures and mistakes don't knock you down. You maintain confidence and resilience in the face of challenges and cultivate good training habits. Just like students with a growth mindset develop better study habits, athletes benefit from it too. Seeking self-improvement leads to better training habits because you face and tackle challenges head-on. It makes you adaptable and flexible. Athletes with a growth mindset handle changes like champs. Whether physical, environmental, or emotional, they are resilient and can cope with new and unfamiliar situations. This adaptability is particularly valuable for athletes competing in different places or cross-training.

Embracing a growth mindset as an athlete can open up a world of possibilities, helping you constantly evolve and excel in your sports journey. Keep that growth mindset strong, and you'll see incredible progress in no time.

GROWTH MINDSET AND RESILIENCE

The cherry on the proverbial cake is that cultivating a growth mindset will make you more resilient. Just look at some of the world's greatest inventions resulting from resilient thinking and attitudes. Take Thomas Edison, for example, a brilliant 20th-century inventor. He faced countless failures in his experiments, but he never gave up. Instead, he saw each failure as a chance to learn from his mistakes. And guess what? Ultimately, he had 1,093 US patents, including game-changing inventions like the electric light bulb, phonograph, telegraph, and motion picture.

How does having a growth mindset help you develop resilience and grit? It's all about bouncing back from difficulties and pursuing your goals with passion and perseverance. When you have a growth mindset:

- You view challenges as opportunities for learning.
- You persist in the face of setbacks.
- You seek feedback and learn from mistakes.
- You celebrate the success of others.

These are the very qualities that constitute resilience. The growth mindset becomes a weapon to conquer obstacles and make your mark on the world.

A growth mindset helps you deal with self-limiting beliefs. Many of us have self-limiting beliefs that affect our self-esteem, confidence, and happiness. These beliefs often don't match reality or the facts, but they can have a powerful hold on us. According to the dictionary, a belief is something your mind accepts as true or factual, often with an emotional or spiritual sense of certainty. But beliefs don't always require active introspection. Some are so ingrained that we don't even question them. For example, we assume the sun will rise daily without thinking too much about it.

Our beliefs come from past experiences and can be both conscious and subconscious. They exist on different levels within us, making them incredibly powerful and essential to understand. Psychologist Robert M. Williams compared beliefs to filters on a camera. They shape how we see the world and profoundly influence our personality. They affect how we perceive ourselves, our worth, our abilities, and even our place in the world. Beliefs impact almost every aspect of our lives, from our moods and relationships to job performance and physical health.

When beliefs are conscious, we're aware of them. When subconscious, they work behind the scenes without us even realizing it. Recent advances in neuroscience have shed light on the power of the subconscious mind. Research shows that at least 95% of our thoughts and decisions originate from the subconscious. It creates filters that shape our reality; we're often unaware of its influence. Just think about this: the conscious mind processes about 40 bits of information per second, while the subconscious mind processes around 40 million bits per second. That's a huge difference. So, the beliefs held by our subconscious mind have a much greater capacity and influence over how we perceive the world and ourselves.

Imagine stepping into a field to play or train, and you have negative subconscious beliefs about yourself or your teammates. How does that affect you? Understanding the impact of these beliefs is the first step toward breaking free from self-limiting thoughts. By becoming aware of them, we can start to challenge and change them, and having a growth mindset is a great place to begin. It is like this:

- Your beliefs influence how you see the world and the people in it.
- They define what you consider good, bad, true, false, real, imaginary, possible, and impossible.
- Your beliefs can affect your positive or negative view of the world.
- They can even control the actions you take and influence your level of happiness and well-being.

Beliefs are like blueprints for your reality. They help you process the overwhelming amount of information that bombards your senses daily. Without them, you'd be lost in a sea of stimuli. Now, sometimes our beliefs can be false. Just like people in the past believed the earth was flat or that the sun revolved around the earth. We can also have false beliefs about ourselves, and these limiting beliefs can hold us back from positive experiences, opportunities, and relationships.

So, where do these self-limiting beliefs come from? According to Dr. Bruce Lipton, a cellular biologist and author, the subconscious mind's most important programming happens in the first six years of life. During this time, we observe and learn from our environment, especially our parents, siblings, and relatives. The perceptions we acquire before age six become the subconscious programs that shape our lives. Young children primarily operate in brain states called delta and theta, which are below consciousness. In this "hypnagogic trance," children mix the imaginary world with the real world, and their minds absorb information like sponges. Anything that's repeated or reinforced during this time becomes their truth.

Often, a single event or thought from childhood is reinforced by someone in authority—parents, siblings, teachers, or peers. This can lead to self-limiting beliefs that stick with us into adulthood. But the good news is that we can change these beliefs. Understanding and challenging them allows us to rewrite our blueprints and create a more positive and empowering reality. The trick is to see these beliefs as opportunities for growth.

Sports can be demanding, not just physically but mentally too. They have positive effects, but it can be challenging to stick with training, for example. It is common to have bad days. It is easy to give in to a negative mind frame and let negative thoughts win. Take a moment to think about your thinking patterns. Do you relate to any of the following negative thinking patterns?

- All-or-nothing thinking: In this kind of thinking, there are no shades of gray; a situation is either black or white. If you make a mistake, it means you are a complete failure.

- Generalized thinking: Here, you use words like 'can't,' 'never,' 'always,' and other definitive words. You may say things like: 'I always get it wrong.'
- Selective focus: In this case, you pick out only one unpleasant detail and allow it to color your feelings about the whole. You may say, for example, 'My hands hurt when I do pull-ups. I hate pull-ups.'
- Selective memory: Here, you exaggerate how significant an event is and shrink achievements.
- Jumping to conclusions: In this case, you expect the worst outcome and convince yourself that your prediction is fact. For example, 'The last time I ran, it was hard. I am not strong enough to handle my body weight.'

There is hope if you relate to any of the above thinking patterns. A growth mindset will allow you to reframe these thinking patterns into more useful thoughts that can encourage you to be better.

HOW HAVING A GROWTH MINDSET BOOSTS YOUR GAME

Our brains are incredible and can change throughout our lives. This ability is called brain plasticity or neuroplasticity. The brain is particularly prone to changes when we have a growth mindset. Scientists use tools like EEG and fMRI to study the brain. These tools help them see which brain regions are involved in a growth mindset and intrinsic motivation. They have found that the dorsal regions of the brain are connected to the growth mindset, while the mid-brain regions are linked to intrinsic motivation. The brain areas associated with a growth mindset and intrinsic motivation are the ACC and ventral striatum, which play a significant role in how we think, feel, and act.

When you have a growth mindset, it affects your brain processes, and brain processes influence your motivated behaviors. That means you become more motivated, resilient, and willing to put in effort when you believe in growth and improvement. For athletes, having a growth mindset can boost their effort, motivation, and resilience in sports.

One study examined how athletes' beliefs about their abilities can impact their performance. What they believe about themselves matters. In the study, researchers found that some athletes have "entity beliefs." This means they believe their abilities are fixed. It's like thinking, "I'm just not good at this, and there's nothing I can do about it." They have a fixed mindset. Other athletes were found to have "incremental beliefs"–a growth mindset. These athletes believe that their abilities can grow and improve with effort. They might say, "I may not be great now, but with practice, I can improve!" Their beliefs were found to make a big difference in how they performed. Athletes with incremental beliefs tended to do better because they believed they could get better with hard work. These findings indicate that having a growth mindset makes you a better athlete.

GROWTH MINDSET IN ACTION

When it comes to your game, your beliefs play a significant role. What you believe to be true affects how you handle different situations. For tennis players, let's take your serve, for instance. If you think your serve isn't strong, chances are you'll play it safe during matches. You might even half-heartedly work on it during practice, convinced you lack the ability in that area. But, if you don't give it your all, that limited belief will prove itself right, and your serve won't improve much. This is true in research as it is practically.

To enhance your performance, you need a growth mindset. That starts with challenging those self-limiting beliefs. Recognize that they are just thoughts, not undeniable truths. Consider the story of Andy Murray, the tennis legend with 36 ATP titles. He struggled on clay surfaces early in his career, with only 11 wins out of 25 matches. But he didn't let that stop him. After 47 final appearances, he finally won a clay title at the 2015 BMW Open. Since then, his record on clay has been impressive, including victories over top-ranked players like Novak Djokovic.

How did he turn things around? By changing his mentality and reevaluating his beliefs about his abilities on clay. Initially, he saw clay as his weakest surface, but as he gained some wins and confidence, he realized that he could excel. His improved footwork and mindset were crucial to his success on clay. He stopped feeling off-balance and learned to chase down balls effectively. Now, imagine what you could achieve if you let go of those self-limiting thoughts you've held onto, embraced a growth mindset, challenged your beliefs, and worked hard to prove yourself wrong.

Andy Murray is not the only example of what having a growth mindset can do. Bruce Jenner's Olympic victories are a shining example of a growth mindset in action. Despite facing challenges with dyslexia, he learned the invaluable lesson that hard work is the key to success. He didn't let his struggles break him; instead, he used them to become stronger.

Like Jenner, Muhammad Ali defied the odds and became one of the greatest boxers ever. He didn't fit the traditional mold of a champion, but he didn't let that stop him. He knew what appeared to be weaknesses and turned them into strengths. Ali honed his mental toughness and studied his opponents so well that he could predict their next moves, giving him a decisive advantage in the ring.

Mia Hamm is another inspiring example of a growth mindset. She fearlessly embraced challenges and recognized areas in which she could improve. When asked what's most important for a soccer player, she said "mental toughness." That's something valuable for anyone, not just athletes. Hamm's belief that she's not yet the most outstanding player but has the potential to become one truly embodies a growth mindset.

Embracing a growth mindset can lead to extraordinary achievements, while a fixed mindset can hold you back from reaching your full potential. Learn from these examples, believe in your ability to grow and improve, and remember that hard work and a positive mindset can take you far beyond what you might have imagined. Avoid the "what-ifs" and embrace the possibilities of what you can achieve through a growth mindset.

THE PLAYBOOK: KICKSTARTING YOUR MINDSET MAKEOVER

1. Overcome self-limiting beliefs

Limiting beliefs can hold us back and keep us stuck in our comfort zones. They have this sneaky way of inhibiting our personal and professional growth and stopping us from achieving our goals. We often treat these thoughts as absolute truths, even if they're not. But the good news is that you can overcome these beliefs and replace them with optimistic messages. Here's how you can do it:

Step 1: Identify your limiting belief. Start by figuring out your limiting belief. It could be fear of failure, self-doubt, or thinking you're not good enough. Take it one at a time, starting with the biggest one.

Step 2: Realize it's just a belief. Remind yourself that your belief may not be grounded in reality. You've convinced yourself of it, but it's not necessarily true.

Step 3: Challenge your belief. Now that you see it's just a belief, question it. Ask yourself things like: "Is this belief really true? What evidence supports it? Has it always been this way? What if the opposite were true? How would someone successful see this situation?" These questions may seem unusual, but they help you see things from different angles and broaden your perspective.

Step 4: Recognize the consequences. Consider the implications of holding on to this limiting belief. How is it holding you back? What opportunities are you missing out on?

Step 5: Adopt a new belief. Choose one that empowers and helps you grow. It might not be easy, primarily if you've held onto the old belief for a long time, but you can make the shift with courage and determination.

Step 6: Put it into practice. Take action based on your new belief. Condition yourself to believe in your new reality. Visualize the results you want to achieve and send positive signals to your brain. Embrace the new belief wholeheartedly, and watch how it positively impacts your life.

2. Use cognitive restructuring

Remember, changing your mindset is a process that takes time and effort. But once you start challenging those limiting beliefs, you'll open up a world of possibilities and reach new heights. The whole idea of steps 5 and 6 is based on cognitive restructuring. When you find yourself trapped in a loop of fear, anxiety, or self-doubt, that's time to investigate your thoughts. Unchecked negative thoughts can sour your enjoyment of the sport and create a cloud of negativity around you. That's why you must take charge of your thoughts. Also known as cognitive reframing, cognitive restructuring comes from cognitive behavioral therapy (CBT), which was developed by Dr. Aaron Beck back in the 1960s.

Dr. Beck, while studying depression, noticed that people had automatic patterns of negative thoughts. These patterns revolved around how they saw themselves, the world, and the future. This led to the birth of cognitive behavioral therapy (CBT), which is now widely used globally. Cognitive restructuring is a key part of CBT. It involves identifying, challenging, and changing those negative thinking patterns to more positive alternatives. The basis of this technique is the thought-feeling cycle. You might think your feelings directly come from the situation you're in. For example, you feel terrible because you made a mistake. But that's not entirely true. While circumstances play a role, they're not the primary cause of your feelings.

The thoughts that follow the situation–in this case, the mistake–trigger your emotions. Often, these thoughts happen so quickly that you're unaware of them. But whether conscious or not, thoughts come before emotions. Once you have a thought, an emotion follows. Negative thinking leads to negative feelings. And when you're feeling down, your subsequent thoughts are likely to be harmful too. This creates a cycle. If you're not mindful of this process, it can repeat over and over. That's why one mistake can lead to more mistakes in a game. You carry the negative emotions from that initial error into the next play.

So, becoming aware of this thought-feeling cycle is critical. Cognitive restructuring helps you break this cycle. Recognizing and challenging your negative thoughts can reshape your emotions and responses, ultimately enhancing your performance and enjoyment of the game. Cognitive restructuring is a tool that can work wonders for all athletes–including you. It works because it's all about swapping those negative, unhelpful thoughts for positive, constructive ones. Do you know what positive thoughts do? They give your performance a solid boost.

Cognitive restructuring boosts your confidence. When your thoughts radiate confidence, that's precisely how you'll feel on the field–super confident. It gives you improved focus because by mastering your thoughts, you'll gain the ability to zone in on what's happening during games. Consequently, it means that you will have more fun. You will no longer be bashing yourself and filling your head with negativity. Instead, your thoughts will become your cheerleaders, shooting your motivation levels through the roof. You will train harder and compete stronger. Here are three steps you can use to restructure your mind:

- Uncover thought patterns

First, the starting line of cognitive restructuring is all about uncovering those sneaky thought patterns that bring negativity. Remember the exercise you did earlier in the chapter to determine which negative thinking patterns you relate to? You can use the results here. Tune in to your feelings daily by answering those questions. The goal is to be more confident and optimistic when facing situations that usually get you down. So, determine when you're most uncomfortable, negative, or anxious during practices or games.

Once you've marked those "not feeling great" times, pay close attention to what you're thinking during those moments. Jot those thoughts down–a journal might come in handy here. Then, dig into the emotions tied to these thoughts. This should be a tad easier since emotions are what got you on this journey in the first place. Go deeper and ask yourself how you are feeling. Do your thoughts trigger a chain reaction? How is your behavior affected by these emotions? What's the reason behind feeling this way? These insights are gold for the next steps.

- Create alternatives

Now that you've got your current thought patterns all mapped out, it's time to whip up a batch of alternatives–a mental upgrade, if you will. In the last step, you listed your negative thought patterns. Now, rethink your perspective. Consider specific situations where those negative thoughts hit you the hardest and brainstorm a different way to view these scenarios. For example, if pre-game jitters mess with your mind, devise a new angle to tackle them. You can also use general affirmations. These are like your personal pep talks. Imagine chatting with a teammate who needs a boost. What would you tell them? Craft a few positive statements highlighting your strengths and strengthening your confidence.

- Change the script

This is where all the pieces of the puzzle come together. You've identified the when, dissected the what, and brewed up alternatives. Now, you need to put it into action. Take those alternatives you came up with and turn them into daily affirmations. Around five to ten phrases will do the trick. Keep them in the present tense for maximum impact. It may feel cheesy initially, but it works wonders in shifting your self-perception. Some examples include:

I've got this.
I'm a rock star player.
My skills are rock-solid.
I trust myself.
All my hard work is paying off.

Imagine you're gearing up for a situation that generally drowns you in negativity. Armed with your new alternatives, be ready to kick negativity to the curb. Do not wait for the bad thoughts–dive right into your alternatives as soon as you sense that negative cloud approaching. With consistent practice, you'll see those negative thoughts fade and your confidence soars to new heights.

3. Try new things and be persistent

When you step into the unknown, your brain grows. Do not be afraid to explore new territories. Don't run from fears–face them. Ask yourself, "Why am I afraid of this?" Break it down, and those fears will shrink. Be sure to stay with whatever activities you pick up. Persistence is your sidekick. When things get tough, don't give up. Make commitments and stick to them, and keep your goals in sight. Goals are your compass. They steer you in the right direction. Don't forget what you're working toward. Think of yourself like an iceberg. What you see above water is just a part of the story. Effort and challenges, the stuff below the surface, make you strong.

4. Reframe losing

Losing isn't the end of the world. It's a stepping stone to improvement. Learn from it, and you'll come back even stronger. Aim for improvement. Instead of comparing yourself to others, compete with yourself and beat your high score. After a challenge, think back. What could you do better next time? This "self-talk" helps you level up. Remember, it's not all about nailing it every time. Embrace the fun of learning and growing. While at it, change the way you think about winning. Winning's cool, but it's not the only gold star. Effort, focus, and discipline–that's the real champion's toolkit.

5. Handle criticism like a pro

Critiques aren't bad. They're like treasure maps for improvement. Accept them, and you'll keep getting better. When you get feedback, see it as friendly advice. It's like getting insider tips to become your best self.

Generally, never think of yourself as talented, intelligent, or gifted. Describe yourself as always learning, intellectually curious, and motivated to grow. That is what a growth mindset looks like. As an exercise, take some time to think of yourself as an athlete. How do you define yourself? Write down the things that first come to mind, edit them to suit a growth mindset, and figure out areas where you would like to grow. You can ask for support from parents or family members. If they are unsure how they can help you, share the next chapter with them.

CHAPTER 7
FOR PARENTS: SHAPING THE CHAMPIONS OF TOMORROW

Magic Johnson once said, "All kids need is a little help, hope, and someone who believes in them." He was onto something. Every one of us needs help sometimes. This chapter is about helping you help your young athlete along their journey in sports. Think about it–you're like their sports cheerleader, coach, and number one fan all rolled into one. Here, you'll understand just how critical your support is. We'll walk through practical strategies that boost your young champ's emotional well-being and performance on the field.

YOUR ROLE AS PARENTS

As a parent, guardian, or caretaker, pat yourself on the back because you're a big deal in your kids' sports. Seriously, without your cheering and support, many kids wouldn't even get to enjoy sports. Sometimes it's puzzling to figure out what to do in various situations or how to give your child the best sports experience possible. It's like trying to score a goal when the field keeps changing. And with all the advice about what's "good" or "bad" for sports parenting, things can get pretty overwhelming. Being a sports parent is way more intricate than just ticking off a list of do's and don'ts.

Here's the deal: being the ultimate sports parent isn't a one-size-fits-all thing. Kids have different needs, and you're coming into this game with unique experiences. Plus, you and your child will face various situations as they journey through their sports adventure. So, step one is all about tailoring your actions to what your child needs and the experiences you both bring to the table. And how do you nail this? By having regular heart-to-heart chats with your young athlete.

If your child is a sports star in the making, it's your mission to create an environment where they can shine. You've got to be their biggest cheerleader, both on and off the field. That means supporting them and their coach, getting clued in about their sport, and tuning into practices and games. It means realizing that your feedback after those practices and games is golden. Keep in mind your kids are like little sponges. They soak up everything you do, including how you generally react to life. So, creating a positive sports vibe in your family is like hitting a home run. Your actions are a blueprint for how they'll act on the field.

Start setting the tone right from the start of the season. Have a chat about your family's core values and remind your kids about what really matters in life. These values? They should reflect on how they behave during their sports adventures.

Ensure you're not throwing a curveball by putting too much pressure on them. Remember, your main goal is to help them feel happy and confident, not to turn them into little sports machines. As your young athlete grows older, you can tap into some sports psychology tricks to help them. These little gems can be a game-changer when navigating their sports journey.

Remember, you're the MVP in your child's sports story. Your involvement, support, and positive vibes are the secret sauce that turns their sports experience into something truly remarkable. Unfortunately, this also means you must watch how you show up so your behavior does not negatively impact your child. For example, avoid trying to relive your glory days with your kid. We all had our glory days, but attempting to relive them through your kids can bum them out. Keep it real, and let them find their path on the field. They will appreciate it, and you'll avoid some serious frustration.

While at it, remember that wins are cool, but losses and disappointments pack the most valuable lessons. Embrace those moments when your young one loses as opportunities for growth, both in life and sports. And when things don't go as planned, skip the blame game. Don't blame the equipment or the coach. Instead, focus on the silver lining that will help your kids grow stronger.

Volunteering is excellent; just ensure you're not venturing into unfamiliar territory. Your kid's got a coach and a team manager–those roles aren't yours to take over. Give them the space to learn from others, and this is true for conflicts. Keep your kids safe, but let them handle their teammate tiffs. It's a chance for them to learn how to communicate and handle challenging situations.

Keep an eye out for warning signs in your and your kid's behavior, like if they're avoiding you after a game or seem more interested in you than the game. Do this without taking credit for their skills and achievements. And remember not to go overboard with referee complaints or grumbling about coaches and volunteers.

Your job is a complex one. You have to figure out how to be your kid's biggest cheerleader but also their guide on the sidelines. The good thing is that others have done it before you, and you can learn from them.

PARENTS BEHIND THE SUCCESS

We've all heard about Stephen Curry's crazy basketball skills. Well, his dad, Dell Curry, was an NBA player too. But what stands out is Dell didn't push Stephen into basketball. He was all about letting his son find his path. No early morning gym wake-up calls, no force. Stephen says that's a big reason he's such a hard worker today. He owns his work ethic because it was never forced on him. Dad, take note. Let your kids be their own awesome selves.

You can also learn from Patrick Mahomes II. Ever heard of him? Kansas City Chiefs quarterback? Super Bowl champion? Yeah, that guy. His dad, Pat Mahomes Sr., was a pro baseball player, but he's known for something even more incredible–being there for his son, no matter what. He's at every game and never misses a chat before or after. He's all about showing love and trust. His message? "Players make plays, and I love you." It's that simple. Be there, love unconditionally, and trust your kids. That's the secret sauce.

The Super Bowl legend Tom Brady didn't have a dad who played pro sports. But guess what? His dad, Tom Brady Sr., is his hero. And not just because of sports but also because of how he lives his life. Brady Jr. Says he looks up to his dad daily, and there is a lesson for parents in there: be role models. It's not just about what you've done but how you live and what you stand for. That's where the magic happens. Francisco Lindor's father had a similar approach. They used to play catch on a steep hill. It wasn't just about sports but about spending time together and sharing experiences. Lindor's dad was passionate and involved. He wanted the best for his son, and that passion shines through. Every dad is different. Some might be laid back like Dell Curry, others super involved like Lindor's dad. There's no one-size-fits-all formula.

The job is for you to be there for your child. It is the same no matter the sport. We've all marveled at figure skaters gliding across the ice, but Sarah Hughes took it to a new level. When she unexpectedly clinched the gold at the 2002 Winter Olympics, it was more than just victory; it embodied her artistry and daring triple jumps. But here's the twist: her mom played a pivotal role beyond training routines.

Hughes' mom didn't just focus on her triple jumps; she planted a powerful mantra in her daughter's heart: "It's nice to be important, but it's more important to be nice." This advice shaped Sarah's approach to fellow skaters, fans, and life. When life throws curveballs–delayed flights, tough days–Sarah's positive spirit prevails, thanks to her mom's wisdom. Her mom's enduring lessons didn't just lead to medals; they sculpted a champion of character.

The same is true for Sue Bird. Sue Bird's story isn't just about breaking records; it's about shattering expectations. Starting as New York's State Player of the Year, she journeyed through national and international victories. Gold medals from multiple Olympics? Check. But her mom's impact reached far beyond the court. No matter the outcome, Sue's mom was there, arms open for a hug. Consistent support, regardless of success, instilled in Sue unwavering confidence. Inheriting her mom's resilience was the game-changer when the clock ran out too soon. Sue wishes she could possess half of her mom's strength. From the sidelines to her recovery, her mom's backing forged a true superstar.

When discussing legendary sports moms, Wanda Pratt's name stands strong. The "Real MVP," as named by Kevin Durant himself, supported her sons as a single mom through sacrifices that fueled Kevin's remarkable journey. Her impact didn't end on the sidelines; she became a motivational speaker and a philanthropist, showing that support isn't just about the game; it's about life. With a Lifetime movie capturing her journey, she continues to inspire. In moments of doubt, her words cut through, "He has a heart of a true Warrior. This too shall pass." Wanda's devotion and strength exemplify the unwavering force behind every MVP–a mom's love.

The examples are countless, but it makes sense to end this list with Dr. AnnMaria De Mars, who set the stage for her daughter, Ronda Rousey, to become an absolute powerhouse in the world of UFC. AnnMaria paved the way as a pioneering force by becoming the first woman to win a World Judo Championship. Her journey as a single mom, raising Ronda and her sisters, showcased her strength. Ronda's Olympic journey was built on her mom's legacy. From their shared passion for Judo, since Ronda was 11 to her bronze at the 2008 Olympics, AnnMaria's resilience resonated. Her words echo empowerment, "You don't owe anybody else your life, and you don't live your life by other people's expectations." That's the kind of motherly wisdom that carves legends.

These stories remind us that behind every triumph, there's a parent who planted seeds of wisdom, resilience, and unconditional love. These remarkable parents embody the ultimate lesson: it's not just about victories but the character, strength, and heart that the journey molds. In the following section, we will break down the lessons we learn from these fantastic moms and dads to help you figure out how to parent your young athlete. The essence? Let your kids find their own path and work ethic. Be there for them, shower them with love, and show trust. Be a role model in how you live your life, not just what you've done. Engage with your kids and share experiences–it doesn't have to be about sports. And remember, there's no perfect parenting playbook. But by watching these parents, we can pick up some valuable insights.

NURTURING EMOTIONAL WELL-BEING AND FOSTERING MENTAL RESILIENCE

1. Promote intrinsic over extrinsic rewards

You might have wondered about that "everybody gets a trophy" trend in youth activities. Some people question if it truly works, and the thing is, they've got a point worth considering, even though there's more to it. It's not just about the trophies; it's about what kind of motivation they bring. External rewards are like getting something you can touch, see, or show off–like trophies, ribbons, or scholarships. While these outside goodies seem cool, they might not fuel the fire inside your young champs the same way. Plus, if the pressure for those external rewards gets too heavy, it can lead to stress and blues–which is the last thing we want, right?

Instead, flip the game. Focus on what's brewing inside. It's all about intrinsic goals. These inner sparks light up the soul–like teamwork, character growth, and becoming a better person. When young athletes chase these internal goals, they flourish. They give their all, shine bright, and don't need a trophy to feel like champions. Imagine the thrill of having a blast, showcasing their creativity, and feeling totally in charge. These are the real MVPs of motivation. These powerful motivators keep young athletes in the game and pave the path to success.

2. Set goals for young athletes

As a parent, help your young athletes set their sights on the prize. Help them set SMART goals.

- Specific: Get clear on what they're aiming for–like a gymnast nailing those floor routines.
- Measurable: Give it numbers. A runner might aim to shave off a minute from their 5K time.
- Attainable: Keep it real. A baseball pitcher's dream of a perfect game is awesome, but more strikeouts might be a solid goal.
- Realistic: Make sure it's what they truly want. Imagine a swimmer who's all about backstroke, not the medley.
- Timely: Set a doable timeline. Think about goals that can happen soon, not just years later.

3. Use positive communication

As a parent, your words matter big time. Your tone, emotions, and how loud you speak count. Positive communication creates real magic. Even written notes make a difference. There is no need for harsh words. And keep an eye on how your young athletes chat with each other. Encourage supportiveness and redirect any negativity. Remind them to cheer on their teammates. You're not just building their sports skills but crafting character and teamwork.

4. Focus on the process, not the outcome

You might have your eyes set on big goals for your young champs, like snatching that championship trophy or taking down a rival team. And sure, those goals can be super motivating. But guess what? There's much more to gain from sports, even if the ultimate victory isn't in the cards. Remind your kids to focus on the journey of becoming better athletes.

Imagine you're coaching a basketball team, and the regional championship is the shiny prize everyone's aiming for. Winning isn't a walk in the park–it takes dedication, hard work, and a lot of skill-building. Plus, you're going to face some fierce competition, no doubt about it. While that championship is the dream, don't forget the steps to get there. Your team might need to up their defensive game, and individual players might need to polish up their free throws. These improvements along the way are like puzzle pieces, crucial to solving the bigger picture of victory. And you can use these specific steps to keep your team motivated as they stride toward that big win.

This isn't just a sports psychology lesson for high school athletes. This idea goes for athletes of all ages, even the pros. When they focus on the process rather than the end result, they're not crushed by setbacks. If the high school team doesn't reach the championships, they can still reflect on their progress, their evolution, and what they've learned.

5. Allow your kid to explore their passions

Maybe you were a sports star back then or a big fan of a particular sport. Your kids might have unique interests and talents. Let them try out different sports and find what lights their fire. Keeping an open mind can lead to some amazing surprises, even if it's not what you expected.

6. Model good behaviors

As a parent, you're a role model on and off the field. Youth sports can get intense, and your kids look to you for guidance. What kind of example do you want to set? Focus on the good stuff, and show them how to respect coaches, teammates, and other parents. Teach them to see the silver lining in every situation, even the tough losses. Instead of getting down about mistakes, show them how to learn and grow from them. Stick to the rules and codes of conduct of the league or club, and lend a helping hand whenever possible.

Encourage your kids to respect the coaches. They pour their heart into developing young athletes. They bring valuable expertise to the game even if they're human and can make mistakes. Encourage your kids to listen to their coaches, follow their guidance, and respect their decisions–even if they don't always agree. Building a positive relationship with the coaches sets an example your kids will likely follow.

7. Teach your kids to lose well and be a good sport

Joining a team is more than just a game–it's a chance for them to learn teamwork and connect with different people.

Negativity and tension can rain on the parade. Teach your kids to avoid bad behavior like trash-talking opponents or dissing other teams. Show them the power of grace in victory and defeat. A few encouraging words can brighten someone's day.

Being a stellar team player is like hitting a home run in life, and it's one of the best takeaways from youth sports. Always praise good sportsmanship and teamwork, not just wins and solo triumphs. Remind your kids that good character and solid attitudes are the true trophies.

8. Watch their diet

Fueling up right is like giving your kids' athletic performance a turbo boost. Keep them hydrated with water, not just fancy sports drinks. Make sure they're on a balanced diet. Think lean protein, healthy fats, complex carbs, and a colorful mix of fruits and veggies in each meal and snack.

8. Help them manage their emotions

Sports bring out a roller coaster of feelings. In one game, they're flying high on a win; the next, they might feel crushed after a loss. Anxiety, anger–it's all part of the game, especially in the heat of competition. As a parent, be their go-to for emotions. Listen to them and let them vent. Let them know their feelings are valid and guide them in turning those negatives around.

Sometimes, they'll need strategies to keep their cool on the field. Simple tricks like counting to five or taking deep breaths can be game-changers. Mind-body practices like these can keep their head in the game during practices and matches.

10. Be proud of them unconditionally

Be their number one fan, no matter the scoreboard. The youth sports journey is about having a blast. Sure, making a travel team or playing in high school sounds grand. College level? The dream. But remember, not everyone's headed for the pros. Your support is the real victory.

Remember, a reminder goes a long way. After practice or a game, high-five them for the effort. Applaud their teamwork. Cheer them on for being awesome humans off the field, like lending a hand with equipment or passing water to a teammate. Remember that sports are more than just the final score–they're a chance for your kids to develop kick-butt habits for life. Keep your eyes on the bigger picture and leave the stress about wins and stats on the sidelines.

Stay engaged, supportive, and positive as you embark on this journey with your young athletes. Your role goes beyond just being a spectator–you're a mentor, a cheerleader, and a source of guidance. Your influence will shape their athletic skills, character, resilience, and outlook on life. Continue to be there for them–celebrating the small wins, offering a shoulder after a challenging game, and reminding them that the journey is what truly matters. Your unwavering support and positive attitude will help your children embrace the world of sports with confidence, joy, and a lifelong appreciation for the valuable lessons it brings.

CONCLUSION

From the chapters of this book, it is clear that the path to athletic excellence is paved not only with physical training but also with the unwavering strength of your mind. Here, you have come across a framework designed to empower you, the aspiring athlete, to rise above challenges and transcend limitations. Throughout these chapters, we've explored remarkable stories of those who have taken their passion for sports and turned it into triumph. From their victories, we've learned that true champions are forged not only in the crucible of competition but in the conquered battle of the mind.

You know for a fact that mental strength is the cornerstone of athletic achievement. The science-backed strategies presented here are not mere theories—they are the tools that will elevate your confidence, sharpen your focus, and, ultimately, carry you to victory. These pages have shown that with dedication, perseverance, and unwavering belief in yourself, you possess the potential to overcome any obstacle and seize your dreams.

As you reflect on the incredible role models who have graced these pages, people like Michael Jordan, Emily Cook, Roger Federer, and many others, remember that their journeys are a testament to the effectiveness of the five strategies in this book. They have harnessed these strategies to ascend to the summits of their respective sports. Their stories illuminate the path you can follow, demonstrating that success is attainable for those who dare to think beyond the limits and cultivate their mental fortitude.

So, whether you stand at the threshold of your athletic career, guide a young athlete's aspirations, or lead a team toward greatness, take this knowledge and make it your catalyst for change. You now have a chance to transform theory into practice, forge your mental resilience, and command the field of play. Armed with the insights within these pages, I encourage you to embark on your own success story. Embrace the Mental Resilience Method, equip yourself with the tools of mental resilience, and march confidently toward your next victory.

The road ahead may be challenging, but remember, you're not alone. Countless athletes have walked this path before, and now it's your turn to join the ranks of champions. As you rise to meet your goals, remember to stay curious, embrace growth, and celebrate every step forward. And as you journey toward greatness, don't forget to share your experiences with this book—your review will inspire others to take the same transformative steps you've taken.

REFERENCES

6 steps to Breaking your Limiting Beliefs. (n.d.). PushFar. https://www.pushfar.com/article/6-steps-to-breaking-your-limiting-beliefs

Amir-Yaffe, G. (2021). 10 Cool Meditations for Pre-Teens and Teens. *DoYou*. https://www.doyou.com/10-cool-meditations-for-pre-teens-and-teens-67578

biglifejournal.com. (n.d.). *Kids and Sports: 5 Effective Ways to Foster a Growth Mindset*. Big Life Journal. https://biglifejournal.com/blogs/blog/kids-sports-growth-mindset

Birrer, D., Röthlin, P., & Morgan, G. (2012). Mindfulness to Enhance Athletic Performance: Theoretical considerations and possible impact mechanisms. *Mindfulness*, *3*(3), 235–246. https://doi.org/10.1007/s12671-012-0109-2

Bishop, I. (2022). Goal setting: How it helps rewire your brain for resilience — Groov | Workplace Mental Wellbeing Platform. *Groov | Workplace Mental Wellbeing Platform*. https://www.groovnow.com/blog/goal-setting-rewire-your-brain-for-resilience

Broadway, K. (2023, June 20). 5 Powerful Benefits of Journaling for Student-Athletes. *NCSA College Recruiting*. https://www.ncsasports.org/blog/benefits-of-journaling-for-student-athletes

BSc, E. H. (2023). What is Goal Setting and How to Do it Well. *PositivePsychology.com*. https://positivepsychology.com/goal-setting

Christino, M. (2021). Mindfulness is the athlete's secret weapon. *inCourage*. https://www.incourage.com/mindfulness-is-the-athletes-secret-weapon

Cohn, P., & Cohn, P. (2020). Sports Visualization for Athletes | Sports Psychology Articles. *Sports Psychology Articles | Sport Psychology Articles for Athletes, Coaches, and Sports Parents*. https://www.peaksports.com/sports-psychology-blog/sports-visualization-athletes

Cohn, P., & Cohn, P. (2023). Murray's Mindset For Playing on Clay | Sports Psychology for Tennis. *Sports Psychology for Tennis | Improve Your Mental Game of Tennis With Sports Psychology Strategies*. https://www.sportspsychologytennis.com/muray-changes-mindset-the-clay

Cpc, K. D. (n.d.). Self-Regulation – A Key Principle for Developing

Resilience. *www.linkedin.com.* https://www.linkedin.com/pulse/self-regulation-key-principle-developing-resilience-cpc

Events, E. (2022). Growth mindset and how it affects athletic performance. *Sports Events in Egypt.* https://www.sportseventsegypt.com/growth-mindset-and-how-it-affects-athletic-performance

Fitness, O. (2021, June 18). 4 Key Journal Strategies for Athletes - OPEX Fitness. *Opexfit.* https://www.opexfit.com/blog/4-key-journaling-strategies-athletes

Fran. (2023, July 20). *What is a growth mindset and how can you develop one? - FutureLearn.* FutureLearn. https://www.futurelearn.com/info/blog/general/develop-growth-mindset

Functional rehab. (n.d.). https://www.functionalrehab.co.uk/blog-posts/performance-limiting-beliefs

Goal Setting: A scientific guide to setting and achieving goals. (2022, August 31). James Clear. https://jamesclear.com/goal-setting

Growth Mindset in Sport and Life: Part 1 | Liv Cycling Official site. (n.d.). Liv Cycling. https://www.liv-cycling.com/global/campaigns/growth-mindset-in-sport-and-life-part-1/24332

Harrington, C. (2023a, March 31). Youth Sports Parenting - 7 Ways to Support Young Athletes. *Jersey Watch.* https://www.jerseywatch.com/blog/youth-sports-parenting-support-young-athletes

Harrington, C. (2023b, June 30). 4 youth sports psychology Exercises to try today. *Jersey Watch.* https://www.jerseywatch.com/blog/youth-sports-psychology

Hirsch, A., Bieleke, M., Schüler, J., & Wolff, W. (2020). Implicit Theories about Athletic Ability Modulate the Effects of If-Then Planning on Performance in a Standardized Endurance Task. *International Journal of Environmental Research and Public Health, 17*(7), 2576. https://doi.org/10.3390/ijerph17072576

Holecko, C. (2021). How to be a good sports Parent. *Verywell Family.* https://www.verywellfamily.com/how-to-be-a-good-sports-parent-4065147

How to set goals like Michael Phelps. (n.d.). https://www.yourswimlog.com/michael-phelps-goal-setting

Hughes, E. (2017). Building resilience through goal setting — MyPLgoals. *MyPLgoals.* https://www.myplgoals.com.au/blog-1/2017/4/25/8li99nyxfg9s29d6gg31j9uzj88109-t8z96

Kuehn, B. (2019, October 29). Your Role as a Parent in Sports. *Vertimax.* https://vertimax.com/blog/your-role-as-a-parent-in-sports

Kuhn, M. A. (2021). How To Teach Youth Athletes To Set Goals. *Stack*. https://www.stack.com/a/teach-athletes-goal-setting

Locke, E. A., & Latham, G. P. (1985). The application of goal setting to sports. *Journal of Sport Psychology, 7*(3), 205–222. https://doi.org/10.1123/jsp.7.3.205

MacLelland, G. (2017, August 24). *Are you a pushy or a supportive sports parent? – Working with Parents in Sport*. https://www.parentsinsport.co.uk/2017/08/24/are-you-a-pushy-or-a-supportive-sports-parent

Magness, S. (2022, September 26). *How to raise a champion – try to relax! – Working with Parents in Sport*. https://www.parentsinsport.co.uk/2022/09/26/how-to-raise-a-champion-try-to-relax

Maintaining emotional control in competitions. (n.d.). Sports Performance Bulletin. https://www.sportsperformancebulletin.com/psychology/sports-psychology-maintaining-emotional-control-in-competitions

Majorian. (2023). Does Visualization Work In Sports? 4 Great Answers - Self Help Motivation. *Self Help Motivation*. https://selfhelp-motivation.net/does-visualization-work-in-sports

Mape, A. (2020). A Mental Training Trick For Athletes. *I Love to Watch You Play*. https://ilovetowatchyouplay.com/2017/03/06/cue-words-can-help-athlete

Metrifit. (2021, March 16). *The importance of goal setting for athletes*. Metrifit Ready to Perform. https://metrifit.com/blog/the-importance-of-goal-setting-for-athletes

Moran, E. (n.d.). *Sport examples of fixed and growth mindsets*. prezi.com. https://prezi.com/rbr-rebf1gub/sport-examples-of-fixed-and-growth-mindsets

Morin, A. (2021). The benefits of journaling for kids. *Verywell Family*. https://www.verywellfamily.com/the-benefits-of-journaling-for-kids-2086712

Ng, B. C. (2018). The neuroscience of growth mindset and intrinsic motivation. *Brain Sciences, 8*(2), 20. https://doi.org/10.3390/brainsci8020020

Orlov, A. (2016, July 14). *Athletes tell all: Why they're thankful for Mom*. Life by Daily Burn. https://dailyburn.com/life/fitness/athletes-grateful-for-moms

Perrelli, H. (2021). Pro Athletes Who Credit Fathers For Success. *Stack*. https://www.stack.com/a/pro-athletes-who-credit-fathers-for-success

Principles of Effective Goal Setting | Association for Applied Sport Psychology. (n.d.). https://appliedsportpsych.org/resources/resources-for-athletes/principles-of-effective-goal-setting

Pushy v Supportive Parents - Free - The Coaching Manual. (n.d.). https://app.thecoachingmanual.com/Content/856

Resiliency. (n.d.). What are the benefits of having a growth mindset for resilience and grit? *www.linkedin.com.* https://www.linkedin.com/advice/0/what-benefits-having-growth-mindset-resilience-grit

Rhew, E. A., Piro, J., Goolkasian, P. E., & Cosentino, P. E. (2018). The effects of a growth mindset on self-efficacy and motivation. *Cogent Education,* 5(1), 1492337. https://doi.org/10.1080/2331186x.2018.1492337

Romana, G. (2020, November 25). Lakers: Phil Jacksonu2019s mindfulness approach to basketball. *Lake Show Life.* https://lakeshowlife.com/2020/11/25/lakers-phil-jacksons-mindfulness

Saini, J. (2023, January 22). How Roger Federer Can Inspire You to Take Control Of Your Anger. *Medium.* https://medium.com/writers-guild/the-calm-and-composed-clan-4f7d535cee14

Spigelmyer, L. (2022). Progressive Muscle Relaxation for Kids (& Adults!) — The Behavior Hub. *The Behavior Hub.* https://www.thebehaviorhub.com/blog/2020/6/8/progressive-muscle-relaxation-for-kids

Sportify It. (2020). 8 Amazing Pro Athlete's Moms Who Deserve All The Credit. *Sportify It.* https://sportifyit.com/8-pro-athletes-moms-who-deserve-all-the-credit

Stankovich, C., & Stankovich, C. (2021). Using Cue Words for Improved Mental Toughness and Athletic Success | The Sports Doc Chalk Talk with Dr. Chris Stankovich. *The Sports Doc Chalk Talk With Dr. Chris Stankovich |.* https://drstankovich.com/using-cue-words-for-improved-mental-toughness-and-athletic-success

Straw, E. (2023a). Cognitive Restructuring Exercise for Athletes. *www.successstartswithin.com.* https://www.successstartswithin.com/blog/cognitive-restructuring

Straw, E. (2023b). Sports visualization techniques for athletes. *www.successstartswithin.com.* https://www.successstartswithin.com/blog/visualization-techniques-for-athletes

The Foundation for Global Sports Development. (2014). Goal setting for young athletes. *Global Sports Development.* https://globalsportsdevelopment.org/goal-setting-young-athletes

Uvpedsadmin. (2021). Resilience Series Part 4: Goal setting. *Utah Valley Pediatrics.* https://www.uvpediatrics.com/topics/resilience-goal-setting

Visualisation techniques in sport - the mental road map for success. (2020). *Discobolul,* 245–256. https://doi.org/10.35189/dpeskj.2020.59.3.4

Waters Creative Ltd (www.waters-creative.co.uk). (n.d.). *Roles of parents in sport*. http://www.sportparent.eu/en/roles-of-parents-in-sport

Webber, D. (2021). Goal Setting in Sport - Importance of Goal Setting for athletes. *Webber Nutrition*. https://webber-nutrition.co.uk/goal-setting-in-sport

Williams, R. (2022, January 6). How Self-Limiting Beliefs Can Sabotage Us (and what to do about it). *Medium*. https://raybwilliams.medium.com/how-self-limiting-beliefs-can-sabotage-us-and-what-to-do-about-it-6adc44fced86

Yeager, D. S., & Dweck, C. S. (2012). Mindsets that promote resilience: when students believe that personal characteristics can be developed. *Educational Psychologist*, 47(4), 302–314. https://doi.org/10.1080/00461520.2012.722805

www.ingramcontent.com/pod-product-compliance
Lightning Source LLC
Chambersburg PA
CBHW052058110526
44591CB00013B/2261